The Ultimate Cash Cow
Turning Hobbies into Cash
(A Pure Profit Technique)

Written by
Steve William Laible, MBA

TKG

The Ultimate Cash Cow
Turning Hobbies into Cash
(A Pure Profit Technique)

Written by
Steve William Laible, MBA

First Edition
©
Copyright 2018

Worldwide Rights Reserved
United Kingdom London Sydney Dublin New Zealand Hong Kong
Mexico City Paris Johannesburg Tokyo Toronto Copenhagen New Delhi
British Columbia India Switzerland Denmark Holland Australia USA

Editor-in-Chief Steve William Laible

Published by
The Kodel Group, LLC
Imprint: Empire Holdings
P.O. Box 38
Grants Pass, Oregon, USA 97528
KodelEmpire.com

Summary: A home-based business model for success. A working thesis which presents a concise, yet thorough overview of the mailing list industry, then guides you through the necessary steps to begin your professional career as a List Broker. Also included, are viable work product reference enclosures. These materials, tips and tools of the trade will further illustrate the mechanics of the mailing list industry, the powerful role direct marketing plays and the integral part you perform as a data collection/dissemination broker.

Library of Congress Control Number: 2018911098
ISBN: 978-1-62485-038-7

Printed in the United States of America, Europe, Asia and beyond...

TABLE OF CONTENTS

PREFACE

Welcome to the Kodel Group.

We're pleased you've shown an interest in becoming an independent mailing list broker. We hope you find the material informative enough to shift your financial stars.

Did you ever imagine '_mailing lists_' could be your ticket to prosperity?

Well, here's what you need to know right out of the gate:

Mailing Lists are real <u>and</u> they're big business.

Direct marketing is a billion dollar industry—and it's growing! Mailing lists play a vital role in this success. Thousands of businesses depend on them to stimulate interest and generate sales.

We've written an innovative business plan, which is at the very threshold of change for the mailing list industry. We expose in detail, the _quiet_ little industry custom of companies selling <u>_your_</u> name for profit, and then reveal how to shift those profits to you instead.

This business model is based on the networking model of exchanging information among individuals or groups creating an exclusive club or buying group, a very powerful force of like-minded consumers. Internet sites are constantly mining data to better understand your behaviors and buying habits. These algorithms micro-target you so businesses can sell more products to you, all the while, profiting in the background by selling your information to others. Others use your online behavior data to sway your votes with their own finely constructed opinions. Oftentimes they appeal to your fears.

INTRODUCTION

Mailing Lists!

Who needs them?

Well, according to Ms. Connie Heatley of the Direct Marketing Association we all do! "This method of marketing," she explains, "has been in existence for 250 years. Ninety-eight million Americans shopped this way last year. It has tremendous consumer acceptance. This is just one-way businesses do business."

So, we at the Kodel Group, began to think, if 98-million Americans shopped this way *in just one year* how many more tens of millions were solicited that didn't respond? That's when the light bulb went on! We felt consumers were collectively losing out on a lot of money they should be entitled to. After all, it is *your* name they're selling back and forth and over again. We thought we could sharpen this marketing tool. But what began as an earnest effort to improve the industry, may in fact, revolutionize it. Our first step was to give the power back to the consumer. We secured the domain, Reclaim Your Name. Then we moved the mailing list brokerage business into the home, making it the ideal home-based business. How well you manage 'information' will be the key to your success.

As we delved more into this industry, we quickly determined traditional mailing list collection methods were simply outdated, rendering them, inefficient, ineffective and costly, especially now that the majority of consumers are fully engaged with the internet. Long before computers and the internet, companies sold your information amongst themselves. This heretofore hidden income stream was and is extremely profitable. This book will enlighten you to an industry you've likely never given a second thought to. The principles set-forth here, can provide you with a path to create your very own successful business.

Have you ever received Privacy Notices, which are required by federal law to be sent to consumers annually? In their veiled narrative, they use the word, "share" which is highly misleading if not outright fraud.

The actual meaning is, "We SELL the information we collect on you." Period!
Sell can also mean, 'rent.'

THE KODEL THESIS

JOB TITLE/DESCRIPTION

PERMISSION LIST BROKER/COMPILER

Throughout this workbook, we use Kodel Group as a means to convey our thesis. You will devise your own business name or group.

As a List Specialist, you seek to collect names, mailing addresses and buying preferences from a very select & powerful group of consumers—those who give their expressed, *written permission* to be included on *mailing lists*, better known as *Permission Lists*. Once your lists are compiled, you then rent them to businesses as an Independent Broker.

The Kodel Group is designed as a buyers' club. Businesses use _our_ permission lists to solicit _our_ members. They are asked to offer their products & services at *deeper discounts*—more than what a traditional direct mail advertising campaign would. Members are <u>never</u> obligated to buy.

Members may also choose to assist the Kodel Group by attracting fresh names for Kodel lists, receiving residual income for their efforts that, in theory, could total in the tens of thousands of dollar range. We make no promises or guarantees however. Everyone's residual income will be different by design. While the effort and commitment levels are different for everyone in business, the opportunities here remain equal. The varying <u>*residual factor*</u> is designed to stimulate the collection of names under the banner, "Reclaim Your Name." [tm]

People providing their names, buying preferences and permission need do nothing further to receive potential discounted offers. They do not have to help assist in collecting more names. They can simply lend their name with permission and do nothing more. They can always choose to become a Compiler or Broker at a later date. Everyone's level of success is defined differently, as it is with any business enterprise.

EXECUTIVE SUMMARY

You can position yourself as a list leader in the billion dollar direct marketing industry. You will serve as an independent Mailing List Broker or Associate Member Compiler, collecting names & consumer information to be compiled into marketing lists and then rented or sold to businesses looking to promote their goods & services via direct marketing.

Compensation is strictly performance based on the number of names collected, lists rented and the residual income generated. Brokers will develop their own business strategies and may rent their lists to other brokers or as many businesses as desired. (*Significant income is generated*.*)

Our business model presents a concise, yet thorough overview of the industry; then guides you through the necessary steps to begin your professional career as a List Broker/Compiler. We've also included viable work product reference enclosures. These materials, tips and tools of the trade will further illustrate the mechanics of the mailing list business; the powerful role direct marketing plays; and the integral part you perform as a data collection/dissemination broker.

---

*One example alone reports *U.S. News & World Report* earns $160,000+ renting out their subscription list. (And they don't just rent it out once.)

YOUR NET WORTH
How Much Are You Worth?

"Pick your own level of poverty and work to stay within it."

WORTHLESS PETE
How much are you worth? Are you rolling in it or are you penniless? Are you somewhere in between? If you can't answer this question, then you've got some reading to do. There is a *right* or *wrong* answer. Knowing what you're worth is important. It sort of puts us on the same page. If you don't know exactly, guess! One last time, how much are you worth? The industry says about four cents!

THAT'S ALL FOLKS
That's all you're worth. Four copper pennies—less than a gum ball.

WELCOME
Welcome to the Mailing List Industry – 101. Please take your seats.

EYE OF THE BEHOLDER
Don't be upset or take it personally. You're just not worth very much! Or are you? If you're a new parent your name commands 25 cents, new homeowners, also worth 25 cents. The *average* consumer *Name List* begins at 4 cents per name & climbs another nickel depending on additional selection criteria, such as, age, gender, telephone numbers, income, etc.

STILL COUNTING
Length of residence fetches another 3 1/2 cents, while dwelling unit size garners 2 1/2 cents more. So when it's all totaled, on average, a *Name List* can get 14-15 cents per name. Then, depending on the output (labels, printouts, sales lead cards or electronic delivery), the cost of each name can increase another penny or three! Whoopee you say! But now your name is worth 18 cents!!! Holler, holler.

BIG DEAL

If you say, "Big Deal" then you might have some self-esteem issues. Try multiplying 18 cents by 5,000 names or 20,000 or 100,000 names and see if that helps. As a mailing list broker, you might be worth millions!

AMERICAN PIE

As you must already know, mailing list companies rent lists with thousands, even millions of names on them. So put on your bib and come get your slice of the God Bless American pie! We're not going to spoon feed you. You'll just have to dive right in—face first. Because if you're really hungry, we're going to show you how to have seconds too and maybe one day, the whole pie!

TECHNIQUE

Keeping the writing style of this book somewhat light and fun, with familiar references or cute plays on words, is meant to keep you interested in the material. There is nothing worse than reading a dry, boring, business book, chocked full of complicated technical jargon. This book has been formatted with a lot of headings to make it cleaner and easier to revisit an area of interest. This is just our teaching technique—way better than 160 page chapters. But please don't let our methods distract you from the message. This is big business, serious business. Okay? We think you'll get more out of the material this way. So just roll with it...

We don't want the material to wash over your eyes, so we've 'home-styled' it a bit to better fit with our *home-based business model*. We have a large audience we're talking to and therefore have to be sensitive to the fact, that not everyone comes from the same business background or enjoys the same life experiences or education levels. We strive to foster warmth and goodwill in our writing style. And yes, sometimes we even try to make you laugh. (Smiles count) 'nuff said...

LEE MARKETING

In 1974, few knew the impact direct marketing would have on business. Yet, it was in that year that Ruthie and Norbert Ewers, with little more than a table to work at, and a _vision_ of the possibilities, founded LEE Marketing Services. At the initial writing of this material, LEE has grown into one of the largest marketing service companies in the nation.

From their state-of-the-art facilities near Dallas, they generate a truly staggering amount of marketing communication (direct mail). With an on-site branch of the U.S. Postal Service and the latest automated equipment, LEE mails *over one million pieces of mail* each and every day!

BUTTERFLIES
It may be too early in the material to get *butterflies* in your tummy, but when it happens, *and it will,* that'll be the beginning of you recognizing the passion and *possibilities!* Having the vision to realize your own potential is an individual one. You have to be excited about this material, about this business, or you're just wasting your time. We're not going to poke you with a stick to get you moving—our job is to give you the information. Besides, if you're excited about something, have passion for it, you won't need anyone to motivate you.

WHET YET
Have we at least whetted your appetite yet? No, then how about this incentive? Do you think a mailing list is *rented only once*? If you do, get a ladder and climb <u>out</u> of the box right now. Expand your thinking. American Business List has rented their mailing lists to over 450,000 clients—more than once. You may want to do the math there...the enormity of scale is undeniable. There aren't even calculators on the market with enough digit display capabilities to express just how much money is generated with mailing lists.

GOLD STANDARD
Permission lists are a new visionary concept that's finally being realized because of social media networking. For decades companies have been mining data to target you. Permission lists can be the gold standard—starting at 25 cents a name if you want. If you're serious and motivated about having your own business, you can become an independent mailing list broker, compiler or associate member.

DING DONG
This isn't Amway, Avon, Tupperware or Mary Kay. There are no start-up kits or products to buy then push onto family and friends. Isn't that refreshing? There aren't any application or franchise fees. This is it! A true Home-Based Business Plan in which to build your empire of wealth.

You simply compile relevant data, shopping habits, etc., and then sell or rent your lists to awaiting, eager businesses, over and over again...

Fortune knocks at every man's door once in a lifetime,
but in a good many cases the man is in a
neighboring saloon and does not hear her."

Mark Twain

You have a fascinating opportunity to adapt the internet and social media networking to create and build your own business. When you gather enough names, you don't have to start your pricing at 4 cents per name. Your Permission Lists can command 25 cents per name based on the very nature and premise of our thesis. The operative word being, permission!

This is what gives your lists value. People who have actually given their written permission to be solicited with deep discounts for goods and services they are actually interested in. But beyond this, when you compile a permission list of consumers who have actually paid a nominal fee to be included on these lists, your lists become pure gold to those businesses looking to do business.

The acquisition cost for attracting new customers can be quite expensive. We can nearly eliminate this expense for them. If businesses can reduce or even eliminate the high expenses associated with all aspects of marketing, print advertisements, television commercials, social media, radio, etc., they can reduce their payroll, ad buys, and by all means lower their cost of goods and services.

Micro-Targeting zeroes in on very specific customers. That alone does not ensure a sale. But if instead, they can zero in on very specific customers who are actually looking for their products, who have given permission, who have paid to be on this exclusive list, you can bet sales will be generated giving businesses a greater return on investment (ROI).

MEET THE PRODUCT
The *product* is Your Name!

THE CATCH
For those doubting Thomases, the catch of the day is, there is <u>no catch</u>. You have the *hook*. Your *name* is the bait. Businesses will bite! You'll be catching retailer bass all day long. They will bite again and again. Eventually, they'll just jump into your boat looking for more bait. Oh, and this is important, there's *"no limit" or seasonal restrictions.*

Businesses that rent lists won't mind being caught because they're hungry. Here's how you satisfy them. Consumers reclaim their name by joining your permission lists. Businesses then rent your lists. Sales are generated. Profits are made. Simple.

By being on Permission Lists, consumers get deep discounts on goods & services, whenever possible, on the purchases they make.

TRUE DISCOUNTS
Since your Permission Lists provide retailers with a more precise targeted mailing list, those consumers who are *actually* interested in their products and services, as a broker, you will negotiate this discount in the terms of the Use Agreement.

[A sample of this agreement is included in this book.]

Retailers are asked to offer your Permission Lists members a true discount. An offer *below what a normal mailing would be for the general public.* And they will do it because you have saved them the expense of wasteful and costly ad dollars as they seek to find or grow their customer base. In essence, you pinpoint their efforts and are rewarded for it. As their new customer, it's up to them to keep you! But this too gives value to our Permission Lists.

SHIFTING

Retailers can afford to offer these savings because shifting random marketing efforts to a more viable, focused, target rich market reduces their costs and produces more sales. Their goods and services reach a more interested and responsive group of consumers. Make sense?

PURE GOLD

Putting your permission lists in the hands of a sales staff is pure gold! It's more than a sales lead, it's more than a cold call or solicitation. It's a permission-based invitation to contact the consumer. This is a real service you are providing. Response rates, sales, and returns on investments (ROI) with respect to ad dollars, commissions, etc., are all much higher, making your lists that much more in demand and valuable! Companies will buy your lists again and again. You can allow businesses to use your lists more than once. You can also restrict the terms. By essentially eliminating cold calls for businesses, which you know can be a big pain for them and you, just wasting everyone's time because of lack of interest on your part, your lists will be in such great demand; it's akin to owning real gold!

RODIN

Auguste Rodin, sculptor of the great *Thinker* statue. Know of it? Well, our first task is to get you *thinking*—as a *consumer* whose name constantly appears on mailing lists whether you like it or not & next, thinking about becoming a mailing list, nay, a permission list broker & business owner. Think with a *business-minded eye*. Understand how pervasive mailing lists are; how *practical & legitimate* they are as a tangible *product*; and how much money they make for their owners. As a broker, you own your lists, your most valuable asset!

HAT TRICK

Is there really a rabbit in that hat or are you using magic? No smoke or mirrors here. But to receive the full measure & intent of what is being presented here, it's important you look at all sides of the industry. That way, you'll better understand the nature, depth, need & purpose for mailing lists & their critical role as a marketing tool. *Case Studies* can oftentimes better illustrate the importance of making a point. So don't overlook reading them at the end of this workbook. They're short, interesting *success* stories. They are included as supporting references meant to motivate you.

HAT RACK

Once this material sinks in, this will all make sense to you.

FIRST HAT

Don the hat of a consumer of goods & services. Has direct marketing ever targeted you? Have you begun to notice how online companies seem to know exactly what you like, have recently searched or purchased? It's like magic huh? These algorithms are being used in smart phones, computers etc., tracking you, collecting data and sharing this data with other companies, even profiting from the sale of this information. Permission lists serve a similar purpose, though not as clandestine. You've essentially already given permission for these online companies to use, share, sell your name, buying habits, searches, etc., or they won't let you use their site. It's a hostage situation. The difference is, you're NOT being compensated for this. We intend to change that!

SECOND HAT

Now wear the hat of a list provider—a mailing list broker. Try to imagine how you will run your business. Who will buy your list? Why is this industry worth billions?

WARDROBE MALFUNCTION

Make a fashion statement by wearing a third hat. See the principles presented here from a 3rd perspective—the ultimate end user—by the businesses who use mailing lists to find you. Why do they use mailing lists and algorithms in the first place? They are profiling you! Knowing more about you affects their bottom line. It's how businesses grow their business.

PERSPECTIVE

This workbook brings to light the quiet little industry custom of companies buying and selling your name and information. They call it sharing but billions of dollars are being made in profits from compiling these lists. Don't you think it's time to Reclaim Your Name and profit instead?

Look at this industry from all three perspectives:

As the _Consumer_;
As the _List Broker_;
And as a Permission List _Business Owner..._

Only then will you better understand the dynamics of the mailing list industry as it relates to direct and online marketing; and how all three feed the process. This knowledge will allow you to carve out your own niche in the giant direct marketing pie and build your own fortune as an independent permission list broker.

DISCUSSION
The Mailing List Industry
(See Status Quo)

THUMBS UP
How are we doing so far? We are aware we repeat some of the same information. It's meant to be redundant so it sinks in. People also tend to skip around rather that read from cover to cover. We don't want you missing anything. When you finish this workbook, we fully expect you to know this industry as well as anyone so you can begin your very own home-based business.

WITHOUT YOU
We are nameless.

TRUTH
This is _not_ a business for procrastinators!

BUSINESS PLAN
This is unlike any business plan or textbook you've read before because we're actually going to teach you how to take back your power and profit from it.

GOAL
The goal is to inform, entertain and expose you to an industry you've probably never given a second thought to—before now.

TASK
The task is to prepare you for a career in the mailing list industry as an independent permission list broker/compiler.

YOUR PERMISSION MISSION
Your mission, should you decide to accept it, is to collect names & non-personal, non-compromising consumer information. It doesn't have to be personal information, general buying habits, hobbies & interests are perfect. This data _and_ the _permission_ consumers are _willing to_ provide gives your lists their power and value.

ROYALTY

Why must we continue to allow companies to profit from selling our names? After all, it is _YOUR_ name they are selling! Shouldn't you be getting the royalties from its use instead? Since no other mailing list company in the world is paying you, we thought we'd make it possible to devise a method for you to profit instead. We've simply _reversed_ it by asking consumers to join permission lists reclaiming their names and getting compensated for their effort while also receiving deep discounts from retailers for being on permission lists.

HUNGRY

Are you hungry for that piece of pie yet? If not, maybe later. If yes, then let's get you off your _low-income_ diet and a place at the head of your own table. Sure, you could skip ahead to the Reclaim Your Name steps portion of this material and learn exactly how to begin making money now. But without the basic understanding, motivation or foundation of this business model for success, you really won't be informed enough or successful enough to make yourself happy and then you'll just blame us. So please be patient. While it's a lot of material to digest, it's really not that complicated once you know the '_recipe_' for success.

ALL FOR ONE

Everyone is a consumer. Their names are already being used and companies are getting rich. This model compensates you. Isn't it about time? As you receive names, your mailing list grows! And so does you piggy bank. When you have a sufficient number of names, you rent these lists to businesses. And for this you get paid—a lot of money—by the businesses renting (or buying) your lists. _Straightforward enough?_

MEMBERS ONLY

Think of it like a buyers' club not unlike Bi-Mart, Sam's Club, Costco, etc., all of which have reoccurring paid-in membership fees which get people in the doors to take advantage of oftentimes lower priced retail products.

You'll want to build a highly exclusive buyers' club with your permission lists. One way to add incredible value to your lists is to build lists only from those who have given their permission. Now, if you build lists where people have also voluntarily paid a small token amount to be on your list, you have now increased the value of your list to the nth power.

It doesn't matter how much anyone pays to join your list, all that matters is they paid something! You never have to reveal this to the businesses you're doing business with, though you can. You simply make the assertion you have

Permission Lists of exclusive members, all of whom have paid to join. Imagine having permission-based mailing lists where consumers have actually paid you to be included on your lists. Think how valuable and marketable your lists have now become. It can be a nickel, a dime, a quarter, even a dollar. You could even build $5 Permission Lists. The more you can get, the more you can charge businesses. The real value is to get something. Permission and a dime can make you rich!

THIS IS YOUR MOMENT

1. Consider establishing a separate email address and maybe even a private mail box (PMB) geared specifically toward you receiving offers. This way permission list offers won't intrude on your regular contact information.

2. Decide how many lists you want to join. (You're always in charge of your data.) Each list you join brings its own unique offers as those brokers will have different business strategies.

3. Set your own budget for each list you join (or offer to others to join). As a broker, you may want to build separate permission lists based on the dominations you receive. If you can build a ten cent permission list, great, but if you can build a one dollar permission list, you will have something of greater value when you begin renting your lists. Imagine owning a $5 Permission List. $20! Solid Gold. But start small. Greed is not consistent with an ethical business.

4. Research what other buying clubs charge. Bi-Mart; Costco; Amazon Prime; Netflix; Sam's Club, etc. Your product is every much as valuable. In fact, more so...because every business wants what you have!

SELL IT

When you begin renting your lists to perspective businesses, you can clearly and honestly state how your lists are compiled (with only those consumers who have given their expressed written permission to be solicited but who have also paid to be added on your lists). In structuring your permission list brokerage business this way, you have essentially created two income streams by collecting the dimes to dollars for inclusion and by renting your lists to businesses.

INTERNET

The internet makes it possible for you to contact millions of people through social media and networking adding them to your list one friend at a time. We highly discourage you using SPAM. Do not contact people you do not know. It will defeat your purpose entirely. The best scenario is to build your permission lists from those consumers seeking you out to be added to your lists. In other words, let them come to you. If you post it, they will come!

BLOGGERS

Maybe bloggers (influencers) already have a worldwide following of consumers but have yet to realize how to fully monetize them. Likely, each of you has many friends or followers on Instagram, Pinterest, Facebook, Twitter, email addresses, etc. This puts you ahead of the game as you already have a small data collection file of unique visitors. This should encourage you, if not propel you to grow your lists quickly and efficiently. You can just begin posting what you're doing.

IN IT TO WIN IT

It's really a race with your other competitors who have also purchased a copy of this book and want to become brokers. Implementation is critical. People (consumers) are encouraged to join more than one list as the offers of deep discounts by businesses will be more pervasive and widespread. Our innovative business model is an industry disruptor shifting the paradigm. Consumers now have a path to take back their power and profit from their participation.

In the end, as a Permission List Broker, it will depend on your timely collection of names, how many and the associated relevant information which make up the quality of your lists. Maintaining supporting documentation is one way to ensure this. Above all else, the information you collect has a shelf-life! You can't expect good results if you rent lists with outdated information, namely contact information. Businesses who rent your lists will not be happy if their marketing efforts are undeliverable. They will never rent from you again and will spread the word within the industry your lists are junk. Be very mindful of this reality.

AGREEMENTS

This workbook contains a sampling of forms, agreements, letters and tips to get you started. As this is your business, you are free to devise additional documents to help sustain, individualize, protect and grow your business.

PARTICIPATION IS GOOD TOO

If becoming a Broker is more than you want right now, you may still choose to become a participating member associate. By sharing your name and consumer information with other broker members, you will still enjoy the benefits of deep discounts whenever they are offered to you.

RECLAIM YOUR NAME

We give our expressed implied 'permission' for you to use our tag lines to attract people to your permission list business. Reclaiming your name is more than a *grassroots* movement—it's a revolution! Well, perhaps that's overstating it a bit. But it is important to have passion in whatever you do. So let's continue...

QUIET LITTLE SECRET

For the general public, mailing lists have been a rather quiet little industry secret. We all know they exist. And for the most part, we accept the custom (business practice) where companies sell the information they collect on you. We are attempting to reveal this industry secret making it possible for you to profit instead, or at least, and to profit as well.

ONE SMALL STEP

Chances are, until this very moment, you've never come close to sitting down and thinking about something as boring or commonplace as '*Mailing Lists.*' Yet here you are, studying them. A great first step! At the very <u>least</u> you will have a better understanding about this industry. At the very <u>best</u> you'll own your own *bank!* A *databank!* And a vault, we suspect, to keep all of those nickels and dimes in!

> *"The difference between a successful person*
> *and others is not a lack of strength,*
> *not a lack of knowledge, but rather*
> *in a lack of will."*
>
> *Vincent T. Lombardi*

CLARITY SAKES ALIVE

For clarity sake, when '*share*' is used in those notices you read online or receive in the mail, it's just a softer way of letting you know they are making huge profits off of your head. The words: share, use, rent, sell are all fairly interchangeable. Established list brokers, firms, financial institutions, publishers, all do it.

THE EDGE

The edge you have over how other mailing lists are compiled is pretty straightforward. Traditional lists are compiled using public domain information. Surely you've received those Privacy Statements from your banks, utility companies or other agencies you hold an account with. Data is collected every time you enter a drawing/contest at a mall; send in a Warranty Card; use a credit card; make purchases online, etc. Even just being inside the DMV database puts your information in the hands of businesses and mainstream mailing brokers who then sell the compiled data to other businesses and financial institutions looking to focus in on you as a consumer. It's all perfectly legit/legal.

The edge you have is gaining the expressly implied and written consumers' permission documented on your Permission List forms! Building your lists by first being granted written permission is about as big as it gets. It's not buried inside a Terms of Use Agreement few of us ever read. It's an implied permission but if you don't agree you don't get to use their website/services. It's more of a hostage or blackmail tactic. Most do offer opt-out options but really, has that ever worked? They still track you!

The second edge (advantage) is your lists are compiled where consumers have paid you something to be included on your particular list. Paying to have their names, lifestyles, shopping habits and hobbies on your list is extremely critical and valuable to you as a broker. This can't be overstated enough. You are bringing businesses a highly captive audience.

When your lists actually generate sales for these businesses, they will have proved their value—to you and the businesses renting or buying your lists. All any business hopes for with mailers is to get a satisfactory response rate. Typically, the national average is only 2%.

MONEY WAYS

Can you guess how many ways money is being made? Two, right? _First_, by the broker selling the list and _second_, by the company who gets sales from the list they've purchased.

WRONG!

INCOME LAYERS

Wrong. There are income layers beyond those. The big boys, the national mailing list houses, draw names from public records, compile them into lists, then sell those lists to smaller brokers (*for a profit*) who in turn sell these same lists to businesses (*for a profit*).

Businesses then generate sales thereby creating their own databases or system of records—consumers who have demonstrated a willingness to buy their products. Wait! Here comes another level. These businesses then "*share*" their lists (you guessed it) <u>with other</u> businesses—*for a profit!*

TANGIBLE VEGETABLE

At every level, they are making a *profit* off of your name! <u>Your Name, I tell 'ya!</u> Do you get that? Therefore, you must think of mailing lists as a *tangible commodity.* Something you can touch. We affectionately call this business practice as:

"Passing your name around like a hot potato for profit!" tm

These national compilers simply extract names from public records and turn them into pure profit. Does it get any slicker than that?

WAIT THERE'S MORE

There's even another revenue stream. A mailing list can become a <u>*by-product*</u> of a company's primary business. For instance, a magazine publisher's primary product is of course, the magazine. *"But wait, there's gold in them 'thar hills."* Publishers have learned to maximize their profits by selling their *Subscriptions Lists* to others.

Subscription Lists are really nothing more than mailing lists of demographically rich gender, age, income levels with specific geographically locations of interested readers. And you thought they made their money only from the magazines or ads.

TAKE THE BAIT

Take a moment. Think more about the above paragraph. Seriously, please don't rush read the material. It's important for you to open your mind to what really goes on in this industry, especially if you are considering becoming a permission list broker. Please do not permit this information to gloss over your eyes. Let it sink in. Think about it, the possibilities this industry offers by making it your own. Say, as an example, this were a fishing magazine with one million paid subscribers. Can you see the potential treasure trove of information available to the publisher; to businesses? Can you visualize the vast number of products and services this type of magazines offers by selling their subscription list to a multitude of companion businesses? This goes far beyond fishing gadgets, lures, bobbers, line, waders, bait and apparel. The point being made here is a publisher can sell their subscription list to a seemingly endless list of suppliers, vendors, (hats, food, pocket vests, socks, knives, boats, reels, waterproof items), vacation / resort destinations (airlines, travel, and lodging), etc. For every business trying to enhance the fisherman's experience is a buyer of this magazine's subscription list!

The only questions are, how hard do you want to work and how rich can you get?

DIMMER SWITCH
We hope the light going _on_ over your head by now means you're starting to appreciate the enormity of this _billion-dollar_ industry & will take mailing lists & their sister, subscription lists, more seriously.

THE 5th ELEMENT
One day, quite by happenstance, it occurred to us, why not create one more revenue source in this industry—one that **benefits you, the 'consumer?'** 'Reclaim Your Name' was born. This isn't just a better mousetrap; this is where the mouse gets to keep the cheese and LIVE!

PURE PROFIT TECHNIQUE
Have you read the _case study_ on **Harry and David** yet? Not unlike a publisher's subscription list, mail order companies generate valuable lists of their own. How valuable do you think their mailing lists are to companies wanting to get their hands on this motivated, cross-section of the buying public—those of us who actually shop this way? How valuable are these lists to the parent company as a _by-product_ of their mail order business? _It's a pure profit technique_. Remember, in crime novels and business, always follow the money.

Marketing is a huge expense and it's growing. If a company acquires thousands or even millions of names as a by-product of doing business then rents/sells those names to other businesses, how much profit do you suppose that is? Smart businesses—maximize profits.

SWIPE IT
Each time you swipe your rewards card you give data compilers access to exactly, precisely what you bought, where and when. Thank you. This data collection is then sold to other businesses helping lower profit margin stores increase and maximize their profits. So take solace in that. You are helping them with their top & bottom lines. You really are a 'valued' customer! Please come again.

While large corporations *spend* millions annually on newspaper inserts, television, radio, and magazine ads in addition to buying mailing lists, others *make* millions off them. While **Home Depot** spends millions, the publisher of <u>U.S. News and World Report</u> makes millions selling their 'Subscription Lists.' Is this a crazy world or what? They sell them over and over and over again to numerous parties, *thereby greatly enhancing their bottom line.* Make no mistake, Home Depot also sells their value customer lists!

<u>AMAZON TWIT FACE</u>

Can you think of other online businesses (of which there are thousands) that might be exacting and extracting your personal and business information, login times, search histories, buying habits, uploaded photos, etc., filling their servers with this compiled data to retrieve, use and sell to others at will? Anyone?

You can do the VERY SAME THING. This is the age of innovation. Are you a trailblazer? You have been given the information, knowledge and secrets, nay, the permission to take full advantage of this industry. Do with it what you will. Being self-employed is a grand idea. This path requires little or no start-up capital. The only inventory is your database. Secure it so it's not stolen. You can use the ideas presented here as the seed of invention to grow your business into something amazing.

<u>USE AGREEMENT</u>

A *Use Agreement* is an agreement (meeting of the minds) terms, costs and conditions, spelling out the details and specifics for both buyer and seller of mailing lists. Such as, will names be for a one-time mailing or multiple mailings? A sample Use Agreement is provided for you to copy, revise, implement or tailor as you choose.

<u>RIDDLE ME THIS</u>
1. How might you go about compiling a '*meaningful*' mailing list in the numbers of names you'll need to make it worthwhile for businesses to rent from you?

2. How many names must you have before it is a considered a list?

3. How will you convince businesses to buy your mailing lists?

4. Why are your lists of value to businesses? (You should already know this.)

5. How are your lists different from other, more traditional lists?

These are questions you'd better have answers to—if not for yourself—then for your prospective clients. They <u>will</u> ask.

WHAT'S YOUR PLAN STAN

How do you intend to generate thousands of names? It ought to be of *interest* to you. It's how you're going to make money. The answer couldn't be easier, *'by word of mouth' via the internet.* But it's critical to lay the foundation first, so you will gain respect for this industry and your business. We'd like you to be successful.

PRACTICE TEST QUESTION

For *practical* purposes, since you're just starting out in the mailing list trade, answer this: To whom might <u>you</u> sell your lists?

ONE TRICK PONY

Okay, that was a trick question. You can't sell a list yet because you don't have a list! Got'cha! So before you can begin selling your first mailing list, you'll have to generate one. (It will help you to know who your end users are before you begin the collection and sorting process. Call it the big picture.)

DOES SIZE MATTER

How small is too small? Our research for this example brings it down to the local level of Anytown, USA. In this case, a local pest control company seeking sales leads paid $300 to the telephone company for a telemarketing list of 5,000 names. At first blush you might think this is affordable. But is it? Paid telemarketers for this company place calls all day long with an extremely high rejection rate manifesting as, not interested, slammed down hang-ups, cursing, etc. This is a dumb way to generate sales. In this case, on average, 50 calls are made before one appointment is set—or about six appointments a day. Why so few?

COLD CALLS

A 'cold' call is when a salesperson places an unexpected call to a home or business. We're seeing in the news more and more where many of these phishing calls are scams making it even more difficult for legitimate business owners to find new customers over the telephone. How many of you have won a cruise or some other prize via a text message or voicemail? Can you see the problem? The call list is not researched. They're just phone numbers. Calls are received unexpectedly & unsolicited. The answering party is usually caught off-guard and has no idea what the call is about until the 'pitch' begins. These calls are oftentimes untimely, unappreciated and unwelcomed or harassing. One day, this sales tool will die off...

NO CALL LISTS

So much a nuisance are these calls, Congress passed a Federal law creating the historic 'No Call' list legislation. It is mostly ineffective. *(But do you see the irony? We need lists to prevent lists!)* Only in America! Many states are following suit. **Limiting** or (underline eliminating) telemarketers from the direct marketing equation is *good* for the mailing list industry and for your business as a broker of permission lists. It eliminates a competitor. You gotta love that. (See Crisis Management)

PEST CONTROL

So, returning to our pest control example and those 5,000 names provided by the telephone company. Can you see any problems with this type of marketing list? Why do you suppose the **response rate** isn't higher than 1 in 50? We'll leave you to ponder this for a minute (tap, tap, tap). Okay, here's a clue: 5,000 names plucked from the telephone pages. Is that *random* or *targeted marketing*?

TEST OUR LOGIC

Pencils down. Go get your telephone book if you even still have one. An old one will do. *(You know we're watching, so just do it.)* Open it. If you have a listed number, turn to it. Look at the information—your name, phone number & maybe even your address. Now from this information alone, do you think anyone else knows if you have bugs or not? Quite the 'random' assumption isn't it?

HOW ABOUT THEM COWBOYS

Try another name unknown to you. At random, flip to another section in the phonebook—any page, any row or column. Put your finger on a name. Can you tell if this person wears cowboy boots? Some marketers toss large nets hoping to catch sales. Is that the best way to do business or go fishing? Is the phonebook a good marketing tool for a business to find new customers? Hardly.

LET YOUR FINGERS DO THE WALKING

Put your finger on one last name. Can you tell what this person's buying habits are, their hobbies or income level? Whether they rent an apartment or are buying a home; if the stork just made a delivery? What sorts of music they like? Well, if you can't do it, why do companies still conduct business this way? This book was written to improve this collection model and change the rules—become a disruptor to this industry by empowering consumers to take back their names.

OUTDATED

We don't subscribe to cold calls or throwing large nets. It's cost prohibitive and wholly inefficient. And we certainly don't subscribe to the use of phonebooks as a valuable source of *consumer* information. These are outdated business models.

THE MORE PRINCIPLE

Assumption Marketing is wasteful, time consuming and a burden on the consumer. In theory, our business model will provide more people with more money at the end of the month—*more disposal income.* See if this basic economic rule makes sense to you. When *more* people have *more* disposable income *more* goods & services are sought. When *more* goods & services are purchased, *more* jobs are created to meet demand. With *more* jobs there is *more* income for us individually, our economy, our government & therefore, less reliance on social programs—trampolines vs. hammocks.

COMMON THREAD
The one common thread that ties together most working class consumers is a simple economic reality—we don't have enough money to all we desire.

We must budget, plan & save and still do without. People just like you are tired of climbing out of debt; clipping coupons; wishing they could buy a new car, new home or take a real vacation. People are tired of making due. How about you?

Most Americans lack the necessary *disposable income* or savings to make purchases on demand. Well, that's not entirely correct is it? How's your credit card debt balances? Spending money you don't have. What a concept. It's like being pinned in a wrestling match; you'll never get out from under making minimum payments. Financial guru, Suze Orman, knows this. It shouldn't take 33 years to pay off a $2500 computer making only minimum payments. We'd like to put forth, with this business plan, an alternative to debt.

"Happiness lies not in the mere possession
of money; it lies in the joy of achievement,
in the thrill of creative effort."

Franklin Delano Roosevelt

TESTING BEGINS NOW
(Keep your eyes on your own work)

TEST #1
Without reading further, take a moment to write down all of the companies you can think of who might use mailing lists. Think outside the box a little. Be brave. Test yourself. Take the time.

Write your answer here:

_____

_____

_____

_____

CANDID CAMERA
Stop! Did you do the above exercise or take a shortcut and just keep reading? We know you're eager but this is a *Business Plan*. Do the work. Your success, in part, is linked to doing what we've outlined. The objective here is to resist shortcuts! We're watching...we're not kidding. We've hidden a micro video chip in the spine of this workbook. We're tracking your every move, page by page. We can see and hear you right now. NSA is a client. So Smile! And for Pete's sake, put a towel on!

GET WOKE
A bit later in the reading the *types of companies* who rent mailing lists will be listed. It's only a small sampling but it should clue you in on how *in demand* mailing lists are. (See Red Hot Tips)

SNOWFLAKES
Like fingerprints or snowflakes, no two lists are exactly alike. Information is not static. It is *always* changing.

*"Information is power and it runs
at the speed of money."*

Steve William Laible, M.B.A.

WARNING WILL ROBINSON

To illustrate just how quickly information changes, compilers use messages like: "Warning, our lists change by 60% each year. Don't use after December 15th, 2018." It's just like a carton of milk. A list can go sour too. Posting an expiration date releases the compiler from deliverability expectations. It also serves notice to retailers—use by the posted date or waste money on an ineffective mailing campaign.

CHANGE OF ADDRESS

For Name Lists, wrong or outdated addresses are bad for business. The retailer sees this as lost sales & rightly so. You keep your email addresses and personal address book and passwords current right? Can you imagine sending out 100 holiday cards & having 60 returned as undeliverable? Outdated information is useless in this industry. It's not good in our personal lives or business.

NATIONAL AVERAGE

Companies clamor for *better mailing lists*. They will seek out your lists if they are effective—higher response rates. That's what businesses want. When that happens, you've done your job. Here's something you likely didn't know or remember, as we did mention it earlier. It's a rather sad story, so grab a hanky. The *average* national response rate is **only 2%**! That's 98% *not* responding. Surely you can do better, right!? (I know, I know, "Don't call you Shirley.") Got it.

RETURN TO SENDER

Unless mail *is not* returnable to sender because of class designations, businesses will track the number of returned mailers. If your rented lists' deliverability is significantly lessened because of *outdated names or addresses*, your client may seek a refund if the undeliverable rate is too high. Or worse yet, never rent lists from you again. They can ill afford to waste a marketing campaign, including postage expenses and labor on undeliverable mail. You can cost them money. Of course on these rare occasions, there are some things you can do to get another chance with them. You can offer them a free or highly discounted 2nd list. Stay current!

YOU CAN'T BE SERIOUS

The lost revenues and time wasted for a client trusting your lists is a cost not recovered from sales. In many cases, these are time sensitive offers. So take your business seriously. Just because it's a home-based business, doesn't mean you won't have an impact on other businesses. Causing a company to lose potential revenue because of inaccurate or outdated lists is not the way to stay in business. Don't sell a two-year old list.

REPUTATION

Your reputation as a list broker will suffer greatly if word gets out on the street that your lists are junk. Credibility and results keep your lists in demand. Produce a quality product. "Repeat business keeps you in business."

DELIVERABILITY

Strive to keep your deliverability rate at least 95%.

FLASH DATING

You have to be aware, the information you collect has an expiration date. People move. They buy homes, have children, change interests which all affect the necessary data buyers of your lists count on. In other words, people go about their lives with zero thought to alerting you about their changes. This is a big problem in maintaining current lists. It would be ideal if those people who fill out their consumer interest forms would show initiative to send you their updated, current information so they can continue receiving deep discounted offers for goods and services. You have to incentivize them! You will have to implement a method to not only purge outdated information but to keep the information you've collected current. The acquisition of constantly adding new consumers to your lists is imperative. But keeping that information current is critical. One suggestion is to devise a FLASH UPDATE system. A loyalty program where people on your lists contact you is the most ideal situation. Perhaps using bulk email notifications, social media or the telephone can be utilized. In the end, this responsibility falls on you. We've got a suggestion for you later in the material.

MEMBERS CAN OPT-OUT

Participating members can always opt-out. Be sure you make this point. Everyone has the option to remove their names and information from your Permission Lists. *Send your check or money order for $950 to the Kodel Group. Attention: Name Removal*, stating your desire to be removed from all system of records. Of course, we're kidding! There is _never_ a cost to opt out. You'll have to make sure it happens immediately. It's the law. You never want to run an unethical business.

PROFIT INCENTIVES

CONNECT THE DOTS

This is first & foremost about collecting names & unique consumer information. The REAL MONEY is in renting your information manifests (lists) to businesses, multiple times. *Since each networking manifest pathway will be different* your permission based database of thousands of names could be joined with other Brokers to really make an impact in the mailing list industry. Some businesses will want 500,000+ names. You'll want to align with other Permission List Brokers!

EQUAL OPPORTUNITY

You have the same equal opportunity to start your own Networking Permission List Brokerage as the next person. Doesn't matter if you're in Rhode Island, New Mexico, Alabama, or South Dakota, the message is the same in every state and Canada: Collect names, manage your information and give businesses more attentive, responsive consumers.

LOTTO FEVER

There's a lot of money to be 'earned' not won. This is not a lottery. Our model isn't about offering *chances* or *prizes* to entice. We most certainly aren't making earning claims, guarantees or promises. This is about making choices & dedicating yourself to making money smartly by Reclaiming Your Name and those of others, working a networking business model with like interests.

BEHAVIOR

Most of us understand the basics of human behavior. This is about collecting as many names as possible. Initially, you may receive some pushback. People are skeptical and cynical as well they should be. Once you establish yourself, this should no longer be a problem. It's not about collecting as much money as possible. This is a business plan for Networking Solutions. Even if you only collect 500 names, by combining with other Brokers, you can grow your business by sharing information. They will, like you, keep the reverse residuals they get with their Consumer Forms. Trust, but verify. How sound are their lists?

WEBSTER
Definition by Merriam-Webster dictionary: <u>NETWORKING</u> (noun): **Exchange of services or information among individuals or groups.** That's our plan!

OLYMPIC DREAM
Is it wrong for the athlete to dream of earning a spot on the U.S. Olympic team, let alone winning a gold medal? Then it shouldn't be wrong for you to dream about winning in business or any other dreams you might have. (It's okay to believe in the beauty of your dreams? It's where your future is.) Without hope, without vision, without implementation, nothing gets accomplished. Nothing!

Our method of getting permission is sure a lot better than the status quo of *stealing names from public records*! The ENTIRE mailing list industry is based on this. (See Status Quo) We can't allow Facebook, Google and hundreds more companies, if not thousands, continue selling our names and information for profit. We are NOT a hot potato. Our sole intention is to shift those profits to you. We're trying to change the status quo. Maverick or visionary, does it matter? We think it's wrong for companies to keep selling your name without your permission to fill their coffers. If you agree with us, then you'll join our movement to change the industry. If you make money as a result, great!

MILLIONAIRE
Nobody expects you to earn a million dollars & over night at that. Or that a million brokers will be out there selling your name. There likely won't be that many people buying this book or learning how to compete with your business. You may be closer to millionaire status than yesterday, especially if you believe in what we are endeavoring to accomplish in this industry and put forth a concerted, committed effort to excel. The first to implement wins the day.

PASSION
You must be passionate & positive about your business. Believing in what we are trying to accomplish is a step in the right direction. Even if you choose another career path, passion must consume you because there is no greater reward in business than being successfully & independently self-employed.

Being self-employed can be exhilarating. Few have this luxury. It is rich with freedoms of time & supervision. Income ceilings don't exist and rewarding achievement bears its own satisfactions and accomplishments. #Independence

There is an excitement in asking yourself for a raise—and getting it.

CRISIS MANAGEMENT

THE BIG PICTURE
Take a macro look at the current business climate and how it may affect the mailing list industry in positive ways. It's all good.

TELEMARKETING
Telemarketers are in real crisis & may soon be extinct, leaving their clients to seek new representation. <u>Mailing lists will likely be the beneficiary</u>. Good news for you, if you're a permission list broker. This is a true growth industry make no mistake about it. Attention telemarketers: This might be the time to consider a career move.

PREHISTORIC
As one industry is collapsing, another is growing. But even the mailing list industry is changing & you'll see how dramatically later in the reading. (Hint: <u>The Courts are involved</u>.) We believe the Kodel Group is at the forefront of change with our permission lists. Telemarketing is a business model akin to dinosaurs roaming the earth on its last leg from India to federal prisons and call centers. Telemarketers are not nearly as effective as they once were because consumers are getting savvier, more assertive, and more resistant. Telemarketers aren't to blame they're just doing their jobs. Who you must blame are those suits behind the scenes using an obtrusive, objectionable and outdated business model. They exist because they do get results. The measure of success is on a downward slope however.

CALL CENTERS
In Oregon, for instance, at this writing, workers in India are answering questions about food stamps & welfare benefits. Oregon has a $24 million contract with an Arizona-based company, eFunds Corp., to administer the Oregon Trail debit card program that disburses food stamps & welfare payments to Oregon residents.

ENGLISH - 101
As part of the contract, the company pays workers at call centers in India to take Oregonians' telephone inquiries about their monthly assistance payments. In many cases, people working in these foreign call centers have to learn to speak English. In many cases, with accents, such as a northerner or southerner, ya'all, in essence to *fool* the caller into believing they've reached an American customer service representative. You're being duped!

PRISON CALL CENTERS

Want to make a camping or RV reservation in a National Park? Could be an inmate you're giving your credit card numbers to. In Oregon, former Secretary of State Bill Bradbury's decision to have state prison inmates staff a new telephone hotline for voters drew criticism. The worry at the time was voters might divulge Social Security numbers or credit card information if inmates asked. This certainly created an atmosphere or opportunity for wrongdoing. Bradbury said, "These fears are unfounded because these inmates are the 'Cream of the Crop.'"

GOOD GRIEF

Is it any wonder then why the telemarketing industry is dying? When the last telemarketer has hung up, you can expect more mailings from advertisers. The growth potential for mailing lists, Permission Lists, specifically, is remarkable.

NAME AND NUMBER PLEASE

Until the telemarketing industry totally implodes, we encourage members to provide telephone numbers on their _Consumer Forms_. Brokers will then have additional clients to rent their lists too. It might be worth taking calls if you're get deep discounts? Telemarketing firms pay very well for telemarketing lists! One list alone can go for $10,000. Not everyone is opposed to receiving calls. Those who have joined your Permission Lists will decide for themselves if they want to give out their telephone number. Legitimate telemarketers will identify themselves as participating in Permission Lists when making their deep discount offers. As any consumer, you don't ever want to give out personal or financial information to anyone calling you. Take the information then Google them or do your own due diligence. An offer must be truly discounted beyond what the general public is being offered. That's the point of being on a Permission List.

GREEN EGGS AND SPAM

One last example of an ineffective business model is internet spamming. Spammers send out tens of millions of daily email offers hoping to pique enough interest to get responses. It's a terrible way to do business because it bothers so many people. Spammers hide behind false pretenses and bounce their unsolicited offers from server to server in vain hoping not to get caught. They are, by in large, not legitimate. Spammers buy lists & choke the system. This alone has hurt the telemarketing industry more than any one thing. There are few sales & no credibility in it. They con (steal) and threaten consumers, especially the homebound or elderly, naive or greedier aspects of human behavior. Soon, this too will be an extinct business cycle. You would be wise not to join the internet spam circuit. Don't out clever yourself. Do the Plan as written!

TREE HUGGER

Even within our own industry we have outdated business practices. Whether you're a tree hugger or not, think how many trees are destroyed with the tens of millions of discarded mailings every day from across our nation, recycling & replanting trees help some. But now, even recycling is being thwarted. The 'bottom line' of any business is important. How much money is wasted printing discarded material? How much money do companies lose in mailing their material? Newspapers are big offenders of waste with all those discarded promotional 'magazine' inserts, usually in weekend editions. Shotgun advertising, whether it's newspapers or mail, is wasteful, expensive and largely ineffective.

CAR-RT-SORT

Receiving Carrier Route Sort (CAR-RT-SORT) _junk mail_ has become so ordinary, so routine & so accepted most people don't give it a second thought. Can you see where a lot of effort, material & natural resources come into play in the mailing list industry? You can convince businesses _there is_ a better way (cost effective) by introducing them to Permission Lists.

VALUE SPIKES

1. Your Permission
2. *Reverse residuals*
3. Making purchases

Value Spike No. 1. Is when you gain the consumer's permission to be included on your lists. Value Spike No. 2. Is when consumers pay to be included on your lists. Think of it as an exclusive buyers' club. We call this a 'reverse residual' where you benefit from them reclaiming their name and they benefit from receiving deep discounts for goods and services. This is the primary selling factor you have to convey. When they join your Permission List Club, they can expect deep discounts greater than the general public receives. This is not to say, they ever have to buy anything. Value Spike No. 3. On those occasions when someone on your lists buys something, you'll add a *third value spike* to permission lists. Anytime the response rate (purchases) for those businesses renting your lists increases, your permission lists gain credibility and value in the industry. The demand for your permission lists increases per name. If your permission lists achieve all three value spikes, you've maximized your lists' value. Businesses will pay more for your Permission Lists if all three are achieved.

PERMISSION LISTS

How are we different? We are a select group of Brokers who offer businesses exactly what they want, a more captive and responsive audience of consumers. Amazon has become such a disrupter over the years yet the deep discounts forecasted with online shopping never really materialized. The concept promise was that online shopping would be far less expensive for businesses than operating brick and mortar stores and therefore they could pass the savings on to customers by lowering their prices. That didn't really happen. There is still a need for businesses to find, attract and keep their customer base. If businesses can micro-target their audience, they can lower their operating costs. There is no guarantee they will lower their prices but in order to get your permission list, that's exactly what they will have to agree to, in writing! (See Use Agreement.)

STANDING TALL

The Kodel Group thesis stands alone! No other mailing list company in the country does what we propose—ask your permission—or help you get deep discounts when your name appears on permission lists. Those 'other' companies passing your name around like a hot potato are soon going to learn, there's a new Sheriff in town.

FAVORS

Permission List Brokers will <u>never</u> require any sort of membership fee or cost associated with adding names to their permission lists. As a consumer, you are doing them a favor by lending your name and consumer information. The industry thinks you're only worth 4 cents. You can show them differently!

PERMISSION NOT GRANTED

Compiling Permission Lists with *only* those people's names who have given their permission may prove to be even more important in the future. Just as Federal and State governments have passed 'No Call' list legislation, courts are just now being asked to prevent companies from selling names where permission *has not* been granted. If this gets enacted, our *Permission Lists* will arguably become the most valuable and sought after lists in the country. <u>We have a huge head start</u>.

SLIPPERY SLOPE

On February 8, 1995, a gentleman, Mr. Ram Avrahami, was interviewed on CBS This Morning, with Harry Smith and Paula Zahn. Mr. Avrahami sued the magazine, <u>U. S. News and World Report</u> for selling his name *without his permission*. In court documents, he alleged the magazine makes over $160,000 for selling its subscription list, yet he receives no compensation. Mr. Avrahami lost his case on a technicality, but the door has been opened. A change <u>is</u> coming.

> NOTE: If you'd like to research this interview further, please contact Burrelle's Transcripts at (800) 777-TEXT or contact CBS Television at CBS Archives, 524 West 57th St., NY, NY 10019.

TRACKING

We suggest <u>saving the original mailing labels</u> of every mailing that identifies you as a Permission List member. This will allow you to track how your association with them is using your name. Members can put themselves on as few or as many lists as they choose. The more lists members are on, the more potential for discounted offers and *reverse* residuals for you become.

AIM HIGH

With higher response rates, Permission List Brokers can get more for their lists & negotiate with companies to offer their goods & services to your members at significantly deeper discounts than a general public mailing.

GOT CLOUT

You'll be earning clout every day as a buyers' club not that unlike COSTCO, Bi-Mart or Sam's Club, where members seek great deals. But unlike these stores, to receive their discounts, you are _required_ to pay a membership fee.

LIST & COMPARE

Earlier you were asked to list companies who buy mailing lists. Did you do your homework or did the dog eat it? (Do you even have a dog?) Refer back to your list & compare. We're pointing you in the _right direction_ for finding new clients.

BRINKS

The types of companies who use mailing lists are seemingly endless! From Insurance Agents to Lawn Care and Landscaping Services. From Security/Alarm System Installers to Credit Card Companies. (Ever get a "pre-approved" credit card offer in the mail?) Your name was SOLD!

WHICH DOCTOR

From Medical Professionals, Dentists & Doctors, Hospitals, Pharmacies & Drug Stores to Refinance & Equity Lenders. From Home Care Centers to Home Improvement Contractors. From Window Treatment Centers to Interior Designers & Furniture Retailers.

BLOCKBUSTER

From Car Dealerships & Real Estate Agents to Diaper Services, & Investment Brokers. From Newspaper & Magazine Publishers to Churches, Clothing Stores, Video & Gaming Rental Stores (while they still exist that is). From Restaurants & Grocery Stores, Hair Salons to Toy Stores, Book Stores & Beyond...Just to mention a few... (See Red Hot Tips)

BACK IN THE BOX

How did your list compare? Did you remain in the box or think outside of it? Who BESIDES businesses use mailing lists?

GOLD SILVER BRONZE

Numerous social & charitable organizations do. Our research shows the United States Olympic Committee in Colorado Springs, rents between _six to nine million names_, _five to six times a year_ in their fund raising efforts. Can you land a visible account with this name requirement? Will you remain on the sidelines or get busy _competing for names_? You don't have to win gold to be considered successful in this industry. Take to heart the following quote:

"If we all did the things we are capable of doing,
we would literally astound ourselves."

Thomas A. Edison

WAX ON WAX OFF

Grasshopper, have you _finally_ figured out why so many companies & organizations rent mailing lists? It's simple really—to make money—the old fashion way—by promoting their goods & services via direct marketing. Companies & organizations use mailing lists to get their messages out. They solicit your business or donation. It can be cost-effective or cost-prohibitive, depending on the list. As you've just seen, it's a fairly endless list of business that rent lists, which is _great news_ for you, as you will have thousands of companies to rent your lists to. Many clients will become repeat customers! Especially when you get them results above the national average of 2%.

BE SPECIFIC MAN

Why is it important to be specific in marketing? So companies can _focus_ in on a _select group of consumers_ ergo yielding a better response rate, which of course, translates into sales & profits. Companies can't waste time or money with mass mailings promoting ballet slippers to the WWE audience—or can they? No they can't. Please don't beat us up. We're just trying to illustrate a point here.

SOPHISTICATION

This business plan has to accomplish more than just telling you what your opportunities are. We have to show you _exactly how to_ compete successfully within a very sophisticated and established industry.

BUY A LIST

Once you have compiled enough names & are ready to find clients to sell or rent your list to consider buying a mailing list from a national compiler. (See Competition) Have them sort by '_small business owners_' or '_new business owners_' _in your area_. You can then contact these businesses & present your permission lists. Key advice: Start slowly. (See Finding Clients below.)

YELLOW PAGES

For the purpose of _finding businesses_ to sell lists to, the Yellow Pages are a great source. You can tell precisely what a business does by their business name, category, description or advertisement. _(The phone book, however, is not a good source for selling to consumers.)_ Can you see the difference?

LICENSING DEPT

You might also want to contact your city or state licensing departments and _request a business list_ for your area. Think they'll charge you? Find out.

QUICKER FASTER EASIER

It can be easier & quicker to buy a business mailing list because the addresses can be printed on mailing labels. You can save a lot of time by not having to rekey the address for 300 labels or 5,000 envelopes. Be mindful of your anticipated response. You can't handle 50 requests for your permission lists yet alone 1750. So grow within your own capabilities. Shoot for just ONE BUSINESS. (You're still a grasshopper after all.) Make your mistakes there, on a small scale. Revise at will, modify, enhance and improve upon your entire system so the next business will receive an even better presentation / offer. Then build your reputation.

FINDING CLIENTS

For the sake of this example, let's say you rented a business list. If you ordered labels, just stick them on _business sized_ envelopes. Include a _short_ introductory letter telling them who you are & why they should rent your Permission Lists. Mention how _everyone_ on your list, 100%, has consented in writing, to receiving mailings of interest to them. Explain further, how this is based on a buyers' club & your members _invite_ offers, especially if savings are more than a general mailing promotion. Tell them also, what your _percentage_ is _(not the dollar amounts)_ of those who have paid to be on your permission list, e.g., 98%. Retailers will be _very_ interested to learn you have a mailing list where people have agreed to offers _and_ have paid to be on your list.

CLOSE IT

When businesses get your letters be prepared & excited to close your first deal. Requests for your permission lists may come pouring in, so be prepared to meet this demand. If the consumer response rates are good & this company makes sales after trying you out, they will be buying lists from you in the future. Imagine them contacting you! So keep collecting names, keep it current and fresh. You won't be able to sell the same old tired list. You're always updating...

PRIORITY ONE

Getting the word out to new businesses that you are a broker with lists to rent ought to be _priority one_ (after securing your list, of course). New businesses are eager to attract customers. They will be pleased to hear what you have to say. What you can do for them. You can help them grow their business by finding that _initial customer base_. It will be their job to keep them as loyal customers. You will be helping businesses generate business. A business owner's time is very limited. Be patient. Follow-up. You are providing both, a service _and_ a product.

HAPPY CLIENTS HAPPY FEET

For lists to have value to _both_ the seller & buyer, lists _must_ produce satisfactory response rates—_the greater the response, the hotter the list_ (by response we mean purchases). To achieve this, the information must be timely, accurate & specific. This is crucial. By providing businesses with 'hot' lists _(where Permission List members make purchases)_, you will have happy clients with happy feet (repeat clients).

MARKETING LISTS

Mailing lists are nothing more than _marketing_ lists from various companies who employ those annoying cold-calling telemarketers pitching their wares via scripts, to your local pizza parlor mailings, election materials, to dentists looking for new patients. Here's what businesses could be saying about your lists:

"Permission Lists: It's how we find customers who don't find us." [tm]

L.S.P.C.

Why are mailing lists so important? _Mailing lists_ are considered '_Leads_' which become '_Sales_' which then become '_Profits_' & '_Commissions._' That's the formula. It's not complicated. (L = S + P + C)

WE WANT ANSWERS

So why on earth would you do anything that might increase your exposure to telemarketers or mailings? It's a fair question you should have already asked & answered by now. TO SAVE MONEY!!!

GOOD INTENTIONS

Our intent is to reduce your <u>unsolicited</u> offers.
Our intent is to change the way you are solicited.
Our intent is to help you RECLAIM YOUR NAME.
Our intent is to see you profit or save instead.
Our intent is to start you on your own business path.

SCRAMBLE

Despite geo-political factors or fluctuations in the economy, direct marketing continues to flourish. The demands for mailing lists are greater today than ever before. Due in part to 'No Call' list legislation, companies who use telemarketers are **scrambling** to find alternative ways to sell their products. Mailing lists are thriving because of costly alternatives such as radio, television & print advertising. Google & Facebook are capitalizing big time on their algorithms which follow your every online click then market to you specifically through their business partnerships. Make no mistake, Google and Facebook are making hundreds of millions of dollars selling ads to businesses which would not be possible or profitable without micro-targeting!

Can you imagine how you'd even build a Permission List before the internet? The internet makes it wholly possible for you to collect names and consumer information just by asking. Of course, you'll want to start with your family and friends and their families and friends, until you eventually have enough names to call it a list worthy of calling yourself a Broker.

SHOULD I STAY OR SHOULD I GO

Mailing lists, though arguably a necessary evil, are here to stay, in one form or another! A targeted mailing list can *pinpoint* a specific audience. But beyond the established status quo of corporations, charitable organizations or small businesses using mailing lists, you might be surprised to learn *even home-based entrepreneurs* are getting into the mix. In addition to using social media, they too are using mailing lists to drive people to their websites seeking customers for their products or services.

Which brings us to the Mitchell Factor...

THE MITCHELL FACTOR

Maybe you're already a businessperson where you're self-employed. You're <u>also</u> a consumer. Maybe a friend or family member is asking you to join their Reclaim Your Name revolution. As a business owner, perhaps one who already uses mailing lists, surely you can see how Permission Lists would be of value to you.

The Mitchell Factor applies to the rest of you who aren't in business necessarily, but have a hobby *(or passion)*, which results in a product or service. Maybe you design t-shirts or collect trading cards or comic books or handcraft interesting wood products, jewelry or sew designer stuff animals or dolls, or beaded designs.

Anything from ties to fishing flies...eBay or craft fairs are not the only way. Maybe instead of a product, you have a talent or skill. A service to your community you can provide, like teaching others to play the guitar or piano. Perhaps carpentry is your skill or yard service maintenance or any number of skills you might possess.

Maybe you use passive newspaper ads to attract interest waiting for customers to find you. Whether beekeeping, bookkeeping, fence building, or any number of specialty skills you possess, you might want to consider buying a permission list.

A targeted permission list with a great slogan will get you business, such as, *Goodwater's Small Engine Repair* –*"If we can't fix it, it's really broken."* Or perhaps you bake pies or cakes or muffins. Maybe you're thinking about operating a food truck. Maybe you're a pretty good bowler and would like to earn some extra money as an instructor. Sure you could hangout down at the alley and get referrals from the Pro or other bowlers but what about all of those sitting at home who would like to learn but just don't know how to get started. A tutor is a wonderful skill.

With smart phones, computers and millions of people not knowing how to use them fully or effectively, if this is your expertise, you could send out a mailing using permission lists offering your services. Stamps are nearly 50 cents a pop, more if you add in prep time, travel time, the cost of the material, envelope. Maybe you're really good at washing windows or have a passion for roses, gardening, growing blackberries, canning or making jam. Whatever your hobby, you can find your audience with micro-targeted permission lists. You can do this. Permission lists are proactive. They can enhance sales of all these goods & services because the response is so receptive. Once you begin networking, the rest is downhill. You simply should not underestimate 'direct marketing.'

LONGING FOR BELONGING
Maslow knew this. Belonging is good—Chamber of Commerce, Rotary, Kiwanas, Elks, Moose, Jaycees, etc. By creating and belonging to a family of permission lists, you will have a built-in customer base of permission list members (looking for great offers) in which to present your products or services. Sales _will be_ greater due to the instant familiarity of your affiliation with permission lists. Networking, it really does work. Granted, the networking of services is more practical within local communities. We doubt the guy in Maine wants his lawn mowed by the guy in Spain. But mailing either a product is very feasible.

THE UGLY AMERICAN
Take the bag off of your head. Show yourself. Don't be ashamed. We are a nation of consumers. Own it! Our overstuffed garages and closets prove it. It's what we do. It gives us pleasure to buy things. It's how we survive as an economy. It may not be right, but it feels SO good. Better to embrace all that it has to offer. As a rich American, you'll be a whole lot more influential in making changes in the world you live in than if residing in poverty. In poverty, all you do is exist. To simply survive is not what you were meant to do on this planet. Don't use social services as a hammock but rather as a trampoline! Start by believing in yourself...

WANTS & DESIRES
What do you think the _primary_ reason is most people don't buy more stuff? Take more trips? Give more to charity? Upgrade their homes? Buy more insurance? Buy nicer things, more often—like appliances, furniture, giant televisions, a first car for their children, send their kids to college? Could it simply be they can't afford it? Is it because we don't have the required _disposable income_ necessary to meet all of our wants, needs or desires, leaving us to make discretionary purchases. With gasoline over $4 a gallon and milk near $4 couldn't you use more money? Stop using credit cards! Spending money you don't have is not a brilliant concept. Paying credit card interest rates of 16% to 26% will keep you down.

DISPOSABLE INCOME
Our business plan, _a model for success_, when properly implemented and followed through with, ought to give you enough disposable income to enjoy more freedoms in your spending. Becoming a Permission List Broker isn't maybe for everyone but it is for some. Adding your name to permission lists can be enough. The discounts on goods and services can make it worth its weight in gold.

LATCH KEY KIDS

Doing _more_ with _less_. Is that what this country is about? How many of you have two or more jobs or those raising children, are both parents working to bring home a paycheck? For the majority of the hard-working middle class, you will not see wage equality in your lifetime, despite the promises from politicians. You will always be faced with cutbacks, layoffs, draw-downs, reductions, budget cuts.

If as a nation, we are working so hard to raise & feed our families and to make ends meet, how much time (or energy) do you have left to volunteer in your community or spend with your family? Do you live for the weekends? What's being neglected in your life? Better yet, who's being neglected? These are serious concerns you probably have but are too busy (or tired) to do anything about.

We strongly believe in what we are doing. Maybe we can help you!

(At some point, _you've got to trust_ what we're saying here. Our research has been extensive in writing this home-based business model for success.)

SHOW ME THE MONEY

This formula—a model for success—just might be what helps you escape your own level of poverty. Homes used to cost $12,000 in your parents' day. Now they are $400,000. What do you think they will be for your children?

The potential is there for everyone. How much can you earn? We wouldn't presume to predict that. No one can. It would be foolish for us & insulting to you to throw out a number. It would also be in poor form. Since you act as an independent broker, we have no direct supervision over you. We aren't there to monitor your performance or check your work ethic. Since there is a *cash* element involved we can't provide testimonials either. We are presenting this material as a means to an end. We really are trying to do business with a handshake.

YOUR INVESTMENT
Unlike other home-based business programs, some costing hundreds of dollars to join, here, you'll make no such investment. You can forget about attending motivational meetings or becoming a double diamond member, because we don't do that either. Buying this book is your only investment, meant to serve as a path.

NEW AND IMPROVED ELIXIR
Unlike those multi-level marketing (MLM) home-based businesses where you are **required** to buy products then promote them; with our business model there is *nothing for you to buy then resell*. This is a very attractive new concept. You won't be pushing those oftentimes, unwanted cosmetics or cleaning products onto your family and friends. There are no soaps, candles, jewelry or parties to attend. No vitamins or health & beauty supplements to unload. No air or water filtrations systems to tap friends with—any of this sound discouragingly familiar?

NAMES & MORE NAMES

All you do is collect names—as many or as few as you wish. That's it. Then you rent those names to an unlimited number of businesses, cashing in on the extremely lucrative mailing list industry with your own newly created home-based business. Of course, when we say 'names' we also mean, 'mailing addresses' and any other consumer specific information you can collect. While we've designed a data collection form for you to use, you may certainly create your own.

WHO DRIVES A PINK CADILLAC

The 'networking' process is *a proven formula*! Consider Avon, Amway, Christmas Around the World, PartyLite, Tupperware & Mary Kay Cosmetics, to mention a few. We've simply made an application for the *information age*. **By adapting** this proven networking process to our business model, you can receive discounts on mainstream products from many more companies & generate a more significant residual income for your efforts.

OBSTACLES

We've eliminated the monetary obstacles of starting up your own home-based business. By creating a co-op, other permission list members fund your business – one dime at a time! Or it could be a buck. This could put you in the enviable position of wealth & power and you don't even realize it yet? And how you get there is actually fun. Our business model is more viable than trendy home parties & better suited to today's fast paced business climate—especially in light of the 'No Call' mood of the nation. We *only want* those people willing to give THEIR PERMISSION. And by no means are we saying you can't host your own permission list parties to gain awareness, acceptance and influence. The more like-minded, agreeable consumers you can attract for your business, the better.

PREMIUM PERMISSION LISTS

For the sake of argument, what if you decided to establish yourself in this industry as a real mover and shaker. You really want to set yourself apart from other brokers. You could set your Permission List entry rate at $5. At this rate, you're not playing around. If you could build a list where everyone paid five dollars, you would be sitting on marketing platinum! When you contacted businesses and shared that you have a mailing list (permission list) where everyone on the list paid $5 to join and are eager to receive their deep discounted offers for goods and services, businesses will jump at your offer to rent your list.

Don't even consider a $20 list but you could. If you could find 500 people willing to pay a one-time voluntary fee of $20, you can be sure they will also keep their information updated so they can continue receiving really deep discounts!

500 people paying you $20 will also bring you a pure profit of $10,000. Imagine if you could collect 10,000 names using social media, like crowdfunding, which is a very real possibility.

Costco collects ANNUAL membership fees for nearly 90 million card-carrying members at this printing! Individual ($60) and 'executive' business ($120) required or you don't get in the door. Most calculators can't even compute just how much that is. Can you? They can command this annual membership fee because their members know they are getting below retail pricing. With the executive membership, members also receive a 2% cash back rewards.

We endeavor to adapt aspects of their proven business model for our purposes. We want to build our permission lists, attract a one-time (or annual) fees (which keeps your lists updated) and then seek out those businesses willing to offer those people on your permission lists a truly steep (deep discount) on their goods and services. Make sense?

A Bi-Mart Advantage family membership is only $5 for life, with a prescription pricing program for hundreds of generic drugs priced from $3.99 to $10.99.

Sam's Club annual membership fee is $45 but they also have 16 membership pricing level add-ons...

All this is meant to show you are the existing ranges so you can establish a price point which is right for your home-based business. It's entirely up to you. As we've mentioned earlier in this workbook, you can create a multitude of lists all with varying buy-in voluntary fees or you can keep it simple.

You might very well only have 500 people on your list in the $5 range. But that's enough names to get started, especially locally. If your list is a general interest list, you will have more options (businesses) you can rent your list too. If you want to get more specific, say, sort your list with only those who golf or play racquetball, or eat pizza, the businesses you contact to rent your list to will be narrower in scope. What makes this thesis work is the people on your list have given their permission and do so because they are genuinely interested in seeing what offers come in. You are effectively saving them money with your exclusive buyers' club.

If it hasn't occurred to you yet, you might want to **buy** a Costco members list and see if they would be interested in joining your unique buyers' club. Brilliant! So remember, you can sort your lists to best serve your marketing needs. You can sort on names, addresses, hobbies and/or how much they paid to be on your lists.

BROKER MANIA

If you think there will be too many brokers out there competing with you, don't. Not everyone buying this workbook will implement it. Not everyone wants to be a broker. Many will just become members by lending their names and consumer data when given the opportunity. This book can serve as a wonderful marketing tool inasmuch as it can, at the very least, expose consumers to our permission list thesis. This will make your job that much easier when trying to build your lists. The concept will already be known. Finding people could be as easy as making yourself known to them as a Permission List Broker. How cool is that?

The more people who become familiar with this business model, the easier it will be to build your lists. If you're the only person who bought this book, you have an even more distinctive advantage by jumping on this business model first giving you a real head start. Everyone coming behind you will be in 2nd, 3rd, 4th place...

Most brokers will start locally. Some will take the next step and expand regionally. Few will take their brokerage nationally. For whatever reasons, those are the realities. You can make your business what you want it to be. We've taken steps in designing collection methods of names ensuring no two lists will ever be identical. That in itself keeps you competitive. Attention to details will set you apart. If you can't manage information, this is not the business for you.

BRANDING

For the sake of branding, may we suggest using Kodel Permission Lists? But you don't have to. Our thought process is, by identifying your lists this way they will become more easily recognizable as you begin attracting members nationwide. However, the downside is, any Broker who provides outdated, undeliverable permission lists, the name, Kodel, could then be stained. There really is no way of protecting the integrity of anyone's list. Maybe on second thought, we'll only use Kodel in our workbook examples. Besides, it might be fun to create your own business name, just be sure you use 'permission list' in your name.

SPREADSHEETS

Brokers, once you begin collecting <u>Consumer Forms</u> it will be necessary for you to capture and transfer the information to a computer spreadsheet program. This allows you to provide sorted/filtered lists to your clients. For instance, you will be able to set a filter to provide the names & addresses of members who have pets, or even more specifically, dogs. You can then begin selling your lists to those types of businesses who target dog owners. (See how easy this is?)

MESSENGER / TEXT / TWEET / PIN / EMAIL FAMILY & FRIENDS

We find this _totally acceptable_. It's a perfect way to quickly expand your name collection methods nationwide. Just be mindful, a local small business isn't likely going to be all that interested in a list with names from several states away, especially if they are counting on foot traffic to their shop.

Resist spamming strangers, okay? Let us repeat this very important instruction: (DO NOT SPAM STRANGERS.) This will not be well-received and could hurt your business in ways you will never recover from. Better to let word of mouth spread throughout social media.

STAND UP

"What did one Mailing List say to the other Mailing List?"

> _"Can I get your name & number?"_

Come on, that's funny. It's way better than a knock-knock joke, right?

FUND YOURSELF

Our business model allows you to create your own Independent Kodel Group Permission List business—without seeking a bank loan. Of course, by Kodel Group, we mean, Smith Group or Jones Group or Anyname Group, the operative word being, 'independent' which is what any self-employed entrepreneur wants.

Our Home-Based Business Model for Success is unique inasmuch as there's no start-up costs, loan approvals, fees, no debt, no interest on debt, no payments. There's no inventory to purchase, nothing to borrow or pay back. Doesn't that sound inspiring? Can you think of another business void of these expenses? Your greatest start-up asset is sweat equity. Just follow the plan. Revise as necessary.

Members can fund their businesses with their nickels & dimes or more. As your business grows, you will need to expand. Hire staff, purchase equipment, mailing list software, even move to a larger facility, etc. In fact, the moment you become a self-made millionaire, you're going to be put on some pretty exclusive lists yourself. You can count on it...

> _"The future belongs to those_
> _who believe in the beauty of their dreams."_
>
> _Eleanor Roosevelt_

PROFILING

Did you know companies *profile* you as a consumer? Whether it's for creditworthiness or something else, it goes on daily. They profile you. Solicit you. *Then sell your name when you're not looking.* Does that seem right? They don't want you finding out how much money they make and they certainly don't want you making a big fuss about it because it gets in the way of cashing their big, <u>pure profit checks</u>. **You're just being used**. It's slight but not insignificant.

SUBTLE
Sometimes the profiling is subtle. The type of car you drive, the price and location of the house you own, or apartment you rent. The hockey stick you just bought with a credit card. We live in an *information age*. It makes sense then for businesses to gather what they can about your buying habits & then solicit you with or without your permission. Start paying attention to those annual Privacy Notices!

PROTECTING YOU FROM YOURSELF
Be sure to follow the instructions for *National Address Removal*. But there's more you can do. Ever fill out one of those shopping mall promotional entries hoping to win a car or boat? If you have, you're putting your name on a *mailing list*. When you buy something over the telephone, you're putting your name on another *mailing list*. When you open a bank account; make travel arrangements; buy new tires or get your car's oil changed; even by subscribing to cable TV, each time you order a magazine subscription or buy something from a catalog, you're putting your name on a list. It goes on an on like that. You're indirectly putting your name on a *mailing list* every single day you engage in commerce. Companies then sell *your* name. Repeatedly! Tell them specifically, DO NOT SELL MY NAME.

SATURATED MARKETS
Is the mailing list world saturated? Does it overlap? Of course it does. But it also doesn't matter. What is being sold is 'information.' And to have any value in commerce, that information has to be timely and accurate. This is a fast paced environment. There is room for you. Do you have the desire? Interest? Passion?

ONE IS A LONELY NUMBER

One name isn't worth very much. Neither is one vote! But collectively, it really matters! Think what 500,000 names are worth—at 4 cents per name. What about 5 million names at 25 cents? Now sell those names over & over.

PIE-IN-THE-SKY

You may think you'll never be able to collect 500,000 names or make that sort of money. But you might be able to collect 2,000 names and sell your lists 100 times for 25 cents per name. Before you know it, you've just sold 200,000 names! This isn't Mt. Everest. (*Have some faith in your abilities, in the process.*)

WALK BEFORE YOU RUN

As with our pest control example, start at your local level. Rent your list to one business. Multiply that by 25 clients a year. More if you're aggressive & full time. Clients will become repeat customers—especially if your lists generate sales.

WHY 25 CENTS

Why will businesses pay 25 cents (or more) per name? Because that's what the industry says they will. It's about demand and results. And that's for a non-permission list. If Kodel members do their part and elevate the response rate above the national average of only 2 percent, the client will have gotten their money's worth. Clients will pay a premium for your permission lists. Strive for greater than 2 percent. If you're on a list, buy something. Every Kodel Group member can facilitate this through a spirit of cooperation. When identified as a Kodel Group member, buy when you can. It helps everyone in the group. Lists become more valuable for everyone.

ASK YOUR CLIENT

Ask you prospective clients what their response rates have been in the past with other, more traditional, mailing lists and then beat that.

RESIDUAL INCOME

Lions & tigers & bears, oh my! Nickels & dimes, quarters & more, oh my! Who knows what residual income you'll receive from all those one-time nominal amounts that come pouring in? Wouldn't it be great if everyone on your permission list sent in $5? Don't expect it. Just be pleasantly surprised. Of course, if you set the fee, then you will not be surprised. And if you decide to use Kodel, like Bi-Mart, an employee-owned business based in different states, the name recognition will be more beneficial in branding on a national level and combining other Kodel lists with Kodel Brokers—a surefire way to add 100x more names to your lists. Larger corporations will require much larger lists, 100,000+ names, etc.

ESCAPE IS NOT AN OPTION

The point is, hundreds of millions of names are being sold or rented over & over again to a multitude of companies. These names have been collected from telephone directories, magazine subscriptions; internet, telephone & catalogue orders; DMV records & yes, even those product warranty cards you fill out.

Additional sources: *Traditional mailing list compilers* tap into:

4,800 Yellow Page Directories; Standard & Poors Directory; State Industrial Manufacturing Directories; City Directory Files; Insurance Company Files; Hospital Directories; Library & School Directories; Government Records; etc.

STOP THE INSANITY

In a collective effort, Kodel Group members can put a stop to this invasion of privacy. **Promote only Permission Lists**. Write your Senator or Congressperson and make the inquiry. Together, we can change the laws. Reclaim Your Name.

THE COMPETITION

If you'd like to learn more about this industry, call the competition. They will assume you are a potential client. Ask them to send you one of their *free* mailing list catalogs. See for yourself what they charge for names. It never hurts to do more research, right? Also, if any of the telephone numbers or addresses have changed since this printing, please call directory assistance, or Google them.

MAJOR LEAGUES
R. R. Donnelley & Son, Metromail   (800) 316-2637
Experian Direct Marketing   (800) 316-2637 Ext. 4321
American Business Information   (402) 592-9000

Info USA   (800) 661-5478
                                      (800) 981-2776

Data Base America   (201) 476-2300

Polk Directories   (800) 606-9290
                                      (800) 275-7655
                                      (800) 221-4112

LEE Marketing Services   (972) 293-5000/5662

SECONDARY INDEPENDENTS
Best Mailing Lists, Inc.   (800) 692-2378
(In Arizona)   (520) 885-0400

R. L. Polk is the largest & one of the oldest list companies in the country. Several smaller, independents: Acquires Total Fulfillment, Phoenix, AZ; Redstone Direct, Omaha, NE; The Rylander Co., Chicago, IL; World Technologies, Omaha, NE; Ace Mailing Services, Atlanta, GA; Trans World Marketing, Freemont, NE. Just to mention a few. You can compete aka Permission Lists! Hello. Innovation!

PRICING YOUR LIST

As a Kodel Group Broker, you set the price for your lists because you have something businesses want, need, and use. Whatever the market will bear, right?

MINIMUM RATE

When renting your permission lists, set a minimum order and rate. Say you only charge $200 per thousand names, set your minimum order at $250. If a company only wants 1,000 names, they'll have to pay the minimum price you set. It's a way to get you more money for your lists. You can adjust for whatever works for you. Be mindful, if you present your lists too inexpensively, it detracts from their perceived and true value. Your clients will meet any price increases you make in the future with reluctance. It's best to set the right price the first time.

HOME DEPOT

Your home-based business can grow beyond your expectations. A small independent Florida brokerage recently filled an order of 1.9 million names for Home Depot. So start collecting names now! Begin working with other Kodel Permission List Brokers so you can achieve a million plus names.

CHESHIRE

When providing companies with your permission lists, you will need to determine in what form they want them. Some companies prefer *ungummed* Cheshire labels for automated machinery they use for mailing in vast quantities. Other clients may choose pressure sensitive (peel & stick) mailing labels. While others prefer galley lists (manuscript form). Some companies prefer the information on a CD-ROM or 3x5 sales lead cards or some other medium.

EQUIPMENT/SOFTWARE

Your capacity to provide all these formats will be limited in the beginning as you're just starting out in business. As you grow, you can justify more equipment & software. Or use available services that can provide the necessary output your clients require. In the meantime, just provide your clients with whatever permission list format you have. Labels are always good. Many national chains who send printed material will want the names and addresses printed directly on the mail pieces. They will track sales and undeliverable mailings. Don't think for one minute you can hoodwink them. You must be results orientated. They are!

CLOSING THOUGHTS

INALIENABLE RIGHTS

As a _consumer_ you have the _inalienable right_ to 'Reclaim Your Name' and profit from its use whether as a broker or buyers' club member; Pursuit of Happiness, right?

PHILOSOPHY

Our philosophy is simple: "The achievement of your goal is assured the moment you commit. To that end, you must engage yourself in the process before you can savor the sweet desserts of your efforts."

ENTREPRENEUR MAGAZINE

According to Entrepreneur Magazine, at this writing, "24 million home-based businesses are up and running. Every 11 seconds someone starts a home-based business with an average **85% success rate**. _Income averages 2-3 times the national average_ and annual revenues reach beyond $401 billion!"

Isn't that encouraging?

It ought to be downright exhilarating! You can do this!

You're starting in a centuries' old established industry with a new, innovative mousetrap. This is certainly far less expensive than purchasing a franchise. The time it will take you to get up and running will also be significantly less.

We wish you great success as an Independent Kodel Group Permission List Broker, Member Compiler, and Buyers' Club Member!

Thank you for your patience, your interest and your attention.

Now get to work...

The Kodel Group, LLC

YOU
Making 2 favorable contacts

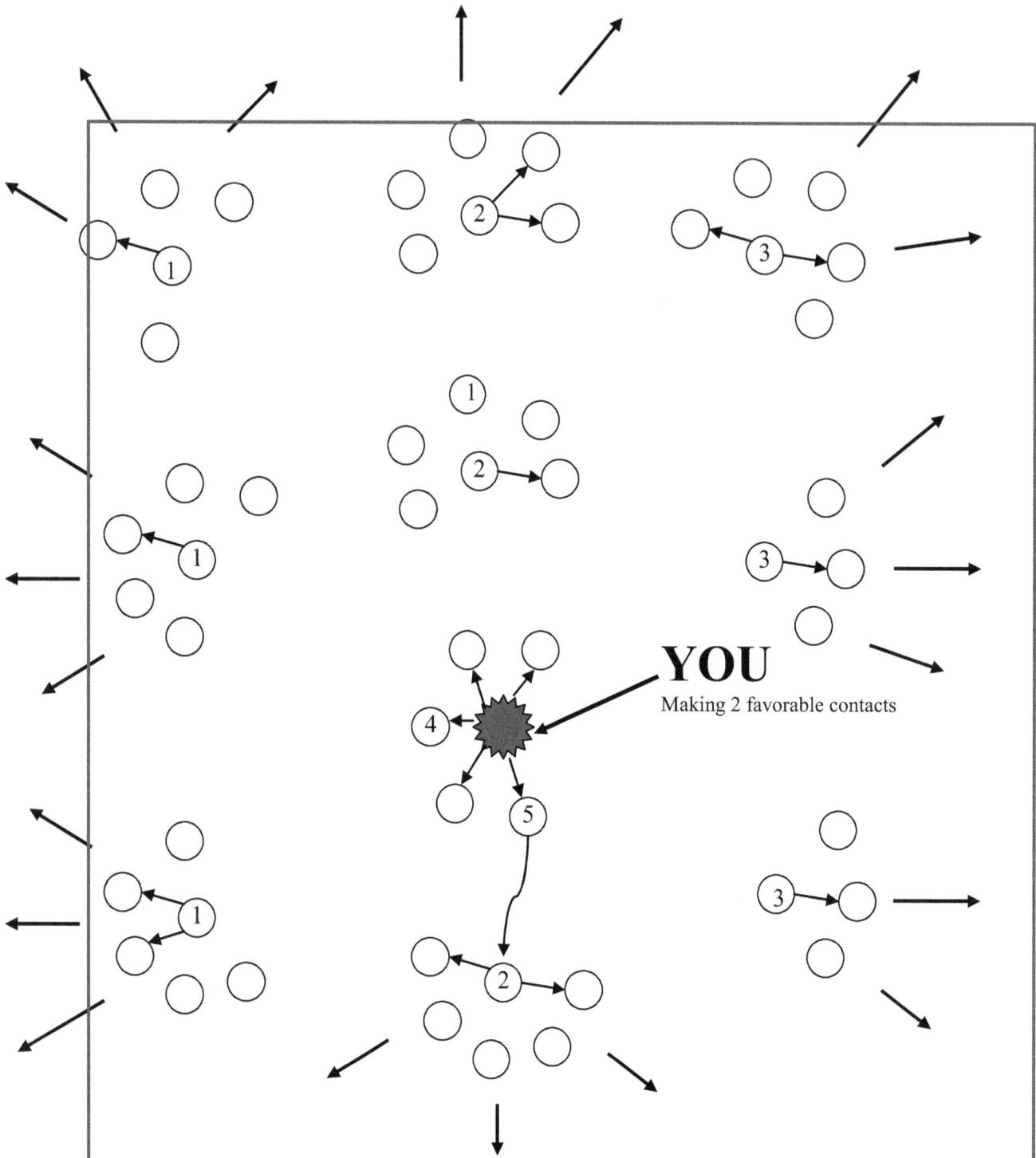

The Kodel Social Networking Explosion Chart
Illustration for example purposes only
Note: Space constraints preclude showing true explosive potential

"Things may come to those who wait…
but only the things left by those who hustle."
Abraham Lincoln

COMMON SENSE CHECK

No one should conclude from the facing Social Networking Explosion Chart for it to go beyond the third or fourth iteration per contact. Some will go more, some less. The expanding factor can never be absolute. Therefore, your anticipated yield will be far less than the example shows. However, in some unique cases, expectations could be greater than expected or anticipated.

Best-case scenario: Three successful contacts might draw in 1,000 _Kodel Consumer Forms_; five, contacts could get you 15,000+ consumer forms; and nine contacts could lead to 500k+ consumer forms to build your lists with. It depends how subsequent members share your post. That's sort of the fun part. Collecting names is <u>only</u> a _means_ to an _end_. The objective here is to compile as many names as possible and then rent/sell those names to businesses. <u>That's where the money is</u>.

Do not expect or anticipate <u>all</u> permission grantors to include a _reverse_ residual with their names as this action is purely voluntary as set forth in this business model. Your actions, and those who continue lending their names and consumer data for your Permission Lists, will set the pace for your eventual success (or failure). Locating like-minded Independent Kodel Group Brokers willing to rent their compiled networking manifests to you at wholesale will help give you the quantity of names you will need to compete successfully as an _independent_ list broker. And in the meantime, you keep trying to add fresh names to your own Networking Manifests. (Another name for Lists.)

'Reclaim Your Name' is an ongoing grassroots effort to amass as many names as possible for the purposes of renting them to businesses as independent brokers. _**Our business model is based on the Social Networking model of exchanging services or information among individuals or groups.**_ Each broker will achieve a different and unique success path based on infinite variables. A broker need only amass as many names as possible and as practical to compile a permission list database.

Pay close attention now to your Ivy League education being shared with you as it relates to our Kodel Group Permission List Brokerage thesis:

HARVARD BUSINESS SCHOOL
NETWORK MARKETING CRITERIA

Network Marketing is being taught in more than 200 colleges, including Harvard Business School. After extensive research into the network marketing industry, Harvard Business School developed three criteria a network marketing company must meet in order to make it a most desirable opportunity. They are:

1. The company must be at least 18 months old, as 90% of all network-marketing companies that fail do so during this period.

2. The company must have a product, which is both _unique_ and highly consumable. Being unique in this case means you have an _exclusive product_ that can only be purchased from the company's distributors. Having a product that is highly consumable means repeated sales, thereby guaranteeing customers loyalty versus a one-time sale having to locate new customers. (See how well Kodel Permission Lists achieve this.)

Research shows loyal customers produce 90% of a brand's profits & _one-time sales create a loss_. The marketing mathematics are persuasive. _It costs 6 to 10 times as much to get a new customer as it does to retain an old one._ But consumers' loyalty isn't for sale. Loyalty requires continued & total satisfaction with a product or service.

3. The company needs to be a 'ground floor' opportunity. Harvard Business School suggests in order for the opportunity to qualify as a 'ground floor' the number of existing active distributors should be less than 1/2 of 1% of the population in the country where this network marketing company exists. If the company has less than 500,000 representatives, you would be on the 'cutting edge' of an excellent opportunity. If the company has less than 100,000 representatives, Harvard Business School considers this to be a 'once in a lifetime' opportunity.

GROWTH

There are four growth stages in a network marketing company:

FOUNDATION

This *usually* lasts 6 months. This is the period when a company develops its product & marketing plan.

CONCENTRATION

This period lasts from 2-4 years when the distributor network is started and grows rapidly.

MOMENTUM

This period lasts from 2-4 years also. This is when the company experiences phenomenal growth. Both retail & distributorship explode in terms of expanding growth. It is during this period that a company virtually sweeps across the nation. When a company's sales reach a certain point, they will reach what is called 'critical mass.' Sales go vertical, right off the charts. Also, approximately 2/3 of the company's growth of new distributors occurs during this period.

HERBALIFE

When Herbalife reached $50 million in retail sales, they jumped to $151 million in only 12 months. They also added over 800,000 new distributors. Let us assume you have an organization, which is producing a bonus check to you of $1,000 per month. When the company reaches 'critical mass' distributors automatically experience a ten-fold increase in their earnings. In other words, $1,000 a month becomes $10,000 per month. *This is the reason for getting involved on the 'ground floor' so you will experience the benefits of explosive growth, should it occur.*

STABILITY

This period lasts for the life of the company. A network marketing company that is dedicated to the success of its distributors will experience longevity, thereby ensuring that an active distributor will realize continued earnings and growth.

INVITATION

We invite your discerning assessment and evaluation of the Kodel Group home-based business model for success and ask that you join us as we turn the mailing list industry on its ear.

PERMISSION GRANTORS CREED

Kodel Group Permission Lists <u>must</u> be supported with the expressed *written consent, including signatures* of <u>all</u> permission list Grantors on the forms mentioned below. This act gives added value (1st value spike) to our permission lists for which Brokers can then command higher negotiated prices, as set forth in the rental Use Agreement.

Such permission extends to the collection of; recording of; storing of; disseminating of; sharing of; renting of; selling of, reproduction of; or otherwise use of information *provided by* Grantors to brokers in the conduct of their legal business. Grantors understand this data will be released to third parties interested in promoting Goods & Services at deep discounts beyond general public offerings. Though *purchases are never required* Kodel Members agree to participate in these offers whenever possible or practical thereby strengthening our permission lists by adding a (2nd value spike). Kodel Brokers endeavor to achieve a response rate higher than the National Average of 2 percent.

Grantors *voluntarily* give information about themselves, which may include but is not limited to, their names, mailing or resident addresses, buying habits, trends, telephone numbers, email addresses or earning, income ranges. <u>All data</u> provided is determined & deemed appropriate by Grantors. Grantors consent for the use of aforementioned information by including their names and addresses on the the *Permission List Authorization Form* **and/or** by signing their *Kodel Consumer Forms*. Grantors may opt-out at any time for any reason but must alert the Broker of Record so their information can be scrubbed from their lists.

Realizing that any 'reverse residual' amount adds a (3rd value spike) to permission lists, Grantors acknowledge they own the <u>right</u> to use their own names & benefit from its use and therefore exercise this *choice* to include a reverse residual *of any or no amount* when giving their permission & providing consumer information.

Permission List Grantors accept the premise for the use of their name and provided information and fully expect to receive offers for goods and services at deep discounts from retailers which go beyond general public offerings.

THE KODEL GROUP
(HOT POTATO - FOR PROFIT)

5 Steps to 'Reclaim Your Name'

Use the included forms, letters & agreements in your business as required.
The information contained in this book is informational only. It will help you in devising your own forms, with attracting consumers to join your permission lists and give you a Broker's Assessment of the required steps necessary to implement your business model for success.

STEP ONE – READ
Read Workbook & Case Studies

STEP TWO – COMPLETE FORMS
Revise, Implement as needed.

STEP THREE – MARKETING
Advocate "*Hot potato for profit*"
'*Reclaim Your Name*.'
Have a Permission List Party

STEP FOUR – ACTION
Collect *Kodel Consumer Forms* as Broker of Record

STEP FIVE – RENT YOUR LISTS
Frame Your First Dollar.

NOTES
1. *Kodel Consumer Forms*

Examples: ✓
☐ I have included a <u>one-time</u> reverse residual of: <u>$5.00</u>
☐ I have included a one-time reverse residual of: <u>25 cents</u>
☐ I have <u>not</u> included a reverse residual.

2. **Any amount** adds a value spike. While amounts are encouraged, they are _**never**_ required! You will receive varying amounts from joining members. That's the fun part. It adds up fast. Use _reverse residuals_ to fund your business, (equipment, facilities, mailing list software, staff, etc.). As much of this may be in cash, keep good accounting records for obvious reasons.

3. If sending a check or money order as a reverse residual _make payable_ to the Permission List Broker of Record, not the Kodel Group, though you can if you'd like.

4. When joining members fill out their _Kodel Consumer Form_ provide 'whatever' _consumer information_ _about yourself_ you deem appropriate! Don't be afraid to release this information—it's already out there—making companies rich. It's your turn to shift those profits your way in the form of deep discounts.

5. Be honest/accurate as the offers you receive will be based on this information.
6. Our business model is designed for collecting names with permission only.
7. Brokers, you might also want to frame your first 'Reverse Residual' contribution.

OTHER

- Feel free to modify forms as necessary. Be sure to use your own address.
- We are a grassroots movement to change the mailing list industry. Take control of your name & show national compilers (who have been selling your name all these years, lining their pockets with gold) that you're now in charge now. Have Fun!
- The Kodel Group, LLC grants permission to Member Brokers to use our copyrighted tags, Reclaim Your Name & Hot Potato for Profit in their businesses marketing should they decide to do so.

PERMISSION LIST AUTHORIZATION

Yes, I wish to Reclaim My Name so please add my name to your Kodel Group Permission Lists. I understand & fully appreciate by providing my name & consumer information, I do so freely & without reservation. As such, I hold the Kodel Group proper, its officers, brokers & members, harmless for the use of my self-provided information. I understand *independent* Kodel Group Brokers *may* rent or sell my name & consumer data to 3rd parties for legal business purposes only.

I understand the sole intended purpose for which my name & consumer information will be used is in commerce via marketing lists known as permission lists. I may opt out at any time, (See Right to Revoke). As a Kodel Group member, I *may* also be presented deeper discounts than are normally offered to the general public by businesses using these lists. I am in essences joining an exclusive Buyers' Club.

Any reverse residual monies I receive due to my membership association are for my disposition alone. In collecting names for Kodel Group permission lists, I agree to act responsibly, abiding by the principles of this business model, all laws & the moral clause. As an active and current Kodel Group Member, I agree to update my information, at least annually, as outlined in this business model, (See Flash Updating).

In addition, I also agree to send one (1) copy of my completed *Permission List Consumer Form* to the Kodel Group Broker of Record for file in the Networking Manifest Catalog for other Kodel Brokers to rent, upon request. In the event I upgrade my member status to Broker, I will also execute a signed *Broker's Agreement* & send forthwith to the Kodel Group Broker of Record.

Permission to use my name & consumer information is granted by my signature below:

Date: _____

Signature: _____

Member's Printed Name: _____

Mailing Address: _____

(City/State/Zip): _____

Telephone: (   )_____Email:_____

Mail to the Broker of Record: (Insert Your Address here.)

THE KODEL GROUP PERMISSION LIST
CONSUMER INTERESTS / HOBBIES / CONSENT FORM

Dear: _____   Date: _____
        (Permission List Broker of Record)

Yes, in an effort to <u>Reclaim My Name</u> kindly add my name & consumer information to your exclusive permission lists. I understand this information is given freely (voluntarily) & may be used in commerce. I expect to receive deep discounts from retailers on Goods & Services which are below general public offerings. I agree to update my contact information with you as practical. I may opt out at any time by notifying you to scrub my information from all systems of records. **SIGNATURE:** _____

☐ I have included a <u>one-time</u> reverse residual of: $_____ to enhance the value of your Permission Lists.

☐ I have <u>not</u> included a reverse residual. <u>Buyers' Club Member:</u> <u>Only</u> include what <u>YOU</u> deem appropriate.

Name: _____   Mailing Address:_____

City/State/Zip: _____   Age: ____ DOB:_____ Gender: _____ Smoke?_____

Telephone: _____ Cell: _____ Email: _____

Income Range: _____ Occupation: _____ Favorite TV program:_____

Residence type: (CIRCLE) Single-family; Condo; Mobile; Townhouse; Duplex; Apartment; Other:_____: Own/Buying/Rent

Bi-Lingual Home: (Y/N)____ (2nd Language):_____ Marital Status:_____ Education Level:_____

Children's ages:_____ Use Credit Cards (Y/N):_____ Use Debit Cards: _____ Order from Catalogs (Y/N):___

Shop Online - List top 5:_____Other:_____

Pets: (CIRCLE) Dog/Cat/Bird/Reptile/Fish/Horse/Monkey. Political Party:_____Favorite Magazine:_____

√ Participate on a regular basis or have an interest in (More Checked Items = More Discounted Offers)

01. ☐ Bicycling	16. ☐ Motor Cycling	31. ☐ Running/Walking/Jogging	46. ☐ Scrapbooking
02. ☐ Bowling	17. ☐ Casino Trips	32. ☐ Flower Gardening	47. ☐ Racquetball
03. ☐ Beading	18. ☐ Automobile Work	33. ☐ Healthy/Natural Foods	48. ☐ Needlework
04. ☐ Collectibles	19. ☐ Coin Collecting	34. ☐ Wildlife/Environmental	49. ☐ Water Sports
05. ☐ Electronics	20. ☐ Tennis Frequently	35. ☐ Vegetable Gardening	50. ☐ Snow Sports
06. ☐ Hunting	21. ☐ Stamp Collecting	36. ☐ Bible/Devotional Reading	51. ☐ Power Lifting
07. ☐ Crafts	22. ☐ Power Boating	37. ☐ Science/New Technology	52. ☐ Bow Hunting
08. ☐ Travel	23. ☐ Gourmet Cooking	38. ☐ Stock/Bond Investments	53. ☐ Photography
09. ☐ Golf	24. ☐ Artistic (#60)	39. ☐ Recreational Vehicles	54. ☐ Camping/BBQ
10. ☐ Hiking	25. ☐ Cultural/Art Events	40. ☐ Entering Sweepstakes	55. ☐ _____
11. ☐ Shooting	26. ☐ Home Workshop	41. ☐ Self-Improvement	56. ☐ Wine/Beer
12. ☐ Antiquing	27. ☐ Avid Book Reader	42. ☐ Science Fiction	57. ☐ Fishing
13. ☐ Fashion	28. ☐ Home Decoration	43. ☐ Real Estate Investing	58. ☐ Vegetarian
14. ☐ Computer	29. ☐ Military Veteran	44. ☐ _____	59. ☐ Charities
15. ☐ _____	30. ☐ MP3/IPod Music	45. ☐ Foreign Travel	60. ☐ _____

Favorites: Color: _____ Number: _____ Season: _____ Meat: _____Vegan: (Y/N) Store:_____

Chips: _____ Cookie: _____ Ice Cream: _____ Cereal: _____ Candy: _____

Car: _____ Truck: _____ Motorcycle: _____ Apparel / Shoe Brands: _____

Beer: _____ Wine: _____ Liquor: _____ Soda: _____ Snacks: _____

Sports/Play: _____ Team/Watch: _____ Hobbies: _____OTHER:

_____

Send (1) <u>copy</u> of this Completed/Signed Form to Your Broker of Record: Company/City/State/Zip

BROKER AGREEMENT

I agree to act as an *independent* Kodel Group Permission List Broker. I understand there is no fee or cost for becoming a broker. I understand as a Broker, I may rent or sell names & consumer data to 3rd parties for legal business purposes only, thereby holding the Kodel Group, LLC proper, its officers & members harmless of all actions resulting from the use of collected consumer information. I have read the liability disclosure & disclaimer statements.

I agree to collect names & consumer data for my own permission lists. I will not employ spamming. I agree to act responsibly, abiding by the principles of this business model, all laws & the moral clause. A signed <u>Permission List Authorization Form</u> and/or a signed <u>Kodel Group Consumer Form</u> will support all persons on my lists & a copy of *both* forms will be sent to the Kodel Group proper.

I understand the sole intended purpose for which names & consumer information will be used in commerce via marketing/mailing lists is known as permission lists. In renting these lists, as a Broker, I will attempt to negotiate with businesses so members *may* be presented deeper discounts than are normally offered to the general public. As stated in the <u>Use Agreement</u> I will inform businesses to identify individuals as Kodel Group Members in all solicitations.

Any reverse residuals, royalties, commissions, or monies received from renting/selling my compiled Kodel Group permission lists are for my disposition alone. I agree to these terms as indicated by my signature below:

Signature: _____ Date: _____

Broker's Name: _____(Please Print <u>all</u> information)

Mailing Address: _____
(Street, City/State/Zip):

Telephone: _____ Email: _____

Fax: _____ Cell: _____

Mail signed document to: The Kodel Group, P.O. Box 38, Grants Pass, Oregon 97528

RIGHT TO REVOKE

Any person who has previously granted permission to be placed on a Kodel Group permission list may revoke or rescind their permission, without cost, at any time, for any reason, or no reason, but must do so in writing.

Submit your name for removal to (insert) Your Company Name / Address:

EXAMPLE:

The Kodel Group
Attention: Name Removal
P.O. Box 38
Grants Pass, Oregon 97528

Your name, address and consumer information will be removed from all systems of records under the control of the Broker of Record.

[As the Broker of Record for the names you collect for your Permission Lists, you'll need a similar form or consumer notice.]

NATIONAL ADDRESS REMOVAL

The following excerpts were provided by the United States Postal Service at our request regarding Mailing Lists:

"...The Postal Service has no authority to compel anyone to remove a name from a *mailing list* and cannot arbitrarily refuse to deliver mail which has the proper postage affixed unless the mailing is sexually oriented..."

"...Direct mail advertisers, responsible for the majority of mailings, use mailing lists containing names and addresses of individuals they believe would be interested in their product. They are nonetheless, unsolicited. Unfortunately, it seems that if a postal customer responds to just one promotional offer, their name appears on additional lists, which are used and *traded* by other mailers. The exchange of these lists is an accepted practice and does not constitute any violation of consumer rights or postal laws..."

"…Some organizations are in the business of maintaining these lists and one of the services they offer is to remove names from lists which are used by direct-mail advertisers. The Direct Marketing Association represents more than 3,600 companies engaged in all aspects of direct marketing. They have developed *voluntary* guidelines for the industry & operate a Mail Preference Service. The addresses for name removal are provided below…"

Author's Note:
By having your name removed from the following national mailing list companies, you are **directly** *adding value* to Kodel Group Permission Lists. This action serves the best interest of all Kodel Group Brokers and Members by inhibiting the *competition's* ability to continue profiting from the sale of *your* name.

RECLAIM YOUR NAME

To have your name removed from these <u>five</u> national mailing list compilers and to enhance your Kodel Group Permission lists, please ask your members to write to:

Mail Preference Service
Direct Marketing Association
P.O. Box 9008
Farmingdale, NY 11735-9008

Advo Systems, Inc.
Director of List Maintenance
239 W. Service Road
Hartford, CT 06120-1280

Equifax, Inc.
Equifax Options Division
Name Removal Department
P.O. Box 4081
Atlanta, GA 30302-4081

Experian
Mail Preference Service
P.O. Box 919
Allen, TX 75013

Trans Union Corporation
National Service Division
111 West Jackson Blvd., Floor 16
Chicago, IL 60604-3595

<u>NO CHARGE</u>
"...There is no charge to remove your name. As a postal customer, you have the right to refuse any piece of mail at the time of delivery, or by endorsing the mailing with the word, 'Refused' in bold print through the address portion of the wrapper. Only letters or parcels for which you must sign are not returnable after delivery has been made..."

<u>STOP THE CALLS</u>
"...To remove your name and help stop telemarketers from calling, we suggest you write to..."

DMATPSD
P.O. Box 9014
Farmingdale, NY 11735-9014

SAMPLE LETTERS

NAME REMOVAL

We have provided sample letters for you to share with your Permission List Membership. If you really want to get their attention, you may also want to cc: Better Business Bureau (BBB), your state Attorney General, Consumer Affairs Division; Federal Trade Commission, Consumer Affairs Department, Congressperson, Senator, etc.

⁄⁄⁄⁄⁄⁄⁄⁄⁄⁄⁄⁄⁄⁄⁄⁄⁄⁄⁄⁄⁄⁄⁄⁄

Date:

Please remove my Name, Address, Home & Cell Telephone Numbers from all systems of records on file with your agency for the maximum allowable period of two to five years.

You ___*do not*___ have my **permission** to use my information for future unsolicited offers to include: Mailing Lists; Subscription Lists; Financial Related or Pre-Approved Offers, Resident Lists; Telemarketing Lists or any other Direct Marketing means or Profiling whatsoever, that your agency may be engaged in.

Please provide verification compliance <u>and</u> written confirmation of my request.

Thank you.

Sincerely,

_____
Your Signature

Name: _____

Mailing Address: _____

Telephone: _____

cc:

SAMPLE LETTER
(Welcome Recruitment)

Dear Prospective Broker,

Welcome to the Kodel Group! You're about to embark on an exciting & rewarding career path. You are always in control of 'your' name and now you'll be able to help others Reclaim Their Names. Our philosophy is put you on a path to success as a List Broker.

We've done the work & extensive research, receiving assistance from several sources & organizations. Do _your_ homework! Study the _Reference Materials_ which will lay the foundation. You'll see what we're doing to change the mailing list industry & how we're shifting the profits to consumers instead.

Everything you need to begin your professional career is provided within this workbook.

We _are_ changing the mailing list industry! We need smart, ambitious, business savvy consumers to embrace our vision. The financial gains can be great. As a final reminder, a primary key to your success is to collect names & consumer information as prescribed in our business model. We've provided you with examples of a data collection _Consumer Form_ & _Agreements_ which you may revise as needed to tailor your business strategies as necessary.

Give this innovative Home-Based Business Model for Success the due diligence it deserves & work in earnest, just as you would any job, with the work ethic & discipline required of self-employment. We truly intend to put you and your business on a path of financial success.

Sincerely,

SAMPLE LETTER
(Initial Recruitment Reply)

Dear Prospective Broker,

Thank you for your interest in becoming an *Independent* Mailing List Broker. We are pleased you have taken the first step. We believe the right background, experience & desire to secure a financial future will make you a valuable candidate.

We *are* changing the mailing list industry! Not only have we exposed the *'quiet'* little industry custom of companies selling *'your name'* for profit we train you quickly & precisely how to shift those massive profits your way instead. Our growth & success, as a national compiler will be as a direct result of our ambitious membership pushing beyond just having entrepreneurial aspirations. This is an exciting, lucrative, fast-paced industry with unlimited growth/earnings potential. How well you manage *information* is the key. It's a simple formula. Collect names & consumer data using our business model. A typical mailing list can rent for $10,000. A brokerage can have sales beyond $200,000 a quarter.

We are looking for *trailblazers!* Successful candidates *must* prepare themselves before representing themselves or launching their new careers as *'independent'* list brokers. Our business-training plan & 'work-product' reference materials accomplish this. Study them. Once we've conveyed our *'Model for Success'* you can begin your professional career as a list broker & change your financial direction—once & for all!

Sincerely,

SAMPLE LETTER
(Initial Consumer Contact)

Dear Consumer,

We 'own' your name! Do you find that alarming, surprising? It's how direct marketing works. Actually, we're just borrowing your name but we did pay a mailing list company to use 'rent' it. They even provided the mailing labels in which to contact you. We're just curious, did they send you a *residual* for using your name in our entrepreneurial endeavors? We didn't think so. We 'rented' your name from a mailing list company to make our point!

We'd like to show you how to benefit from companies selling your name by asking you to participate in our exclusive Permission List Buyers' Club where you will receive deep discounts from retailers for goods and services not normally offered to the general public for just giving your permission to use your name and consumer information. We're asking you to Reclaim Your Name. If you're interested read on...

We *are* changing the mailing list industry! Not only have we exposed the 'quiet' little industry custom of companies selling 'your name' for profit we'd like to see if we can get you some incredible deals in the process. We invite you to join our Buyers' Club by simply filling out the enclosed Consumer Form and consider enclosing a small reverse residual as this will give your List Broker extreme barging power when negotiating discounts for their goods and services.

If you have more questions about the future of Permission Lists and how you too might become a Broker, you can review the bestselling book, 'The Ultimate Cash Cow – Turning Hobbies into Cash – A Pure Profit Technique' on Amazon.

Thank you.

Sincerely,

PRIVACY STATEMENT EXCERPTS

They are not ASKING, they are TELLING you!

- Note: <u>INDUSTRY CODE WORDS</u>: May = Will. "SHARE" = RENT/SELL

<u>R.L. POLK</u> compiles auto registration information for its core list.

<u>Donnelley Marketing</u> compiles names/addresses from 4700+ white pages, auto registrations, drivers' licenses.

<u>WASHINGTON MUTUAL</u>: A now defunct bank: "...We are permitted by law to **share** **all** the information we collect on you with companies that perform marketing services...<u>your name</u>, address, **social security number** & credit history...so they can provide products & services to you...Even if you are no longer a customer, we will continue to treat your non-public information in the same way as if you were still a customer..."

<u>PHILIP MORRIS</u>: "...We won't **share** your name outside our conglomerate of companies..."

<u>MBNA</u>: "...If you tell us ***not*** to **share** information with companies outside of MBNA that wish to offer you their products & services, <u>please understand</u> <u>we</u> <u>will continue</u> to **share** your information to retailers, direct marketers, communication companies, Internet service providers, hotels, travel agents, cruise lines, car rental agencies, airlines, publishers, etc. [Kodel Note: Does this seem right to you? They have no shame in <u>selling your name</u> to increase their bottom line. Well, let's beat them at their own game!]

<u>LES SCHWAB TIRE CENTERS</u>: "...We may share "<u>personal information</u>" **about you** with companies or organizations outside the Les Schwab family..."

<u>USAA</u>: "...USAA collects information about customers & former customers and may **share** it with..."

BANK ONE: "...Information **Sharing** Outside the Bank One Family...We may **share** 'any' of the personal information that we collect about you..."

CHARTER CABLE: "...The Cable Act allows us to disclose your name & address for mailing lists..."

AMERICAN FAMILY PUBLISHERS: "...Mailing List Selection Committee..."

CITIGROUP - TEXACO: "...The law allows us to **share** your transactions..."

PRODUCT WARRANTY CARDS & QUESTIONNAIRES: "...Please complete & return within 10 days...you will receive important mailings & special offers from a number of fine companies..."

YOU GUESS THIS ONE: "...Please be advised your **opt out rights** described below **will not apply** to the **sharing** of information with marketing services & joint marketers..."

- Industry databases & marketing providers include: Student Lists; Credit Card Holders; Mail Order Buyers; Medical Offices; Voter Files, etc., etc., etc.

- If you find any of this distressing or disturbing, we invite & encourage you to join the Kodel Group. Help us change the mailing list industry. We will show you how to laugh all the way to the bank...because the only one profiting from YOUR NAME should be YOU!

Attention
KODEL GROUP Brokers/Compilers/Associate Buyers' Club Members:

- This is exactly what we're talking about!
- Altria Group is the parent company of Philip Morris.
- Philip Morris is a conglomerate with hundreds of subsidiary companies worth billions of dollars!
- (So when they say they won't "share" your name with *non*-Philip Morris companies, does that really mean anything?) - Same goes for Unilever!

- You'll find where these companies write their Privacy Statements as if they are doing you a favor!
- RECLAIM YOUR NAME!

LOYALTY ROYALTY DISBURSEMENT
(Philanthropic Endeavor)

EXAMPLE
POTENTIAL INCENTIVE ENHANCEMENT
For Participating Consumers

This may not be practical but it is worth exploring.

Dear Buyers' Club Members,

At some future date, we hope to implement a _Loyalty Royalty Disbursement Program_ paying (annually) an amount equal to the Reverse Residual amount you included with your Consumer Interest / Hobby Data Form x 10.

Since it's impractical to tally each time a member's name is used on our permission lists, to show our appreciation, we are rewarding you, as an incentive for your participation and annual updates of your current information as follows:

For example purposes only:
If you voluntarily give a $5 Reverse Residual when submitting your Consumer Data Form, we will send you $50 annually as a thank you, if you keep us informed of your updated and current information, including your mailing address, telephone number, email, income range, additions to your family, change in buying habits or consumer preferences. If you provided a $20 Reverse Residual, you'll receive $200! Because without you, we are nameless.

(_Independent Brokers of Record_) You might want to set a ceiling on the Reverse Residual you are willing to pay annually. You might want to consider making a loyalty rewards offer because without them, your business doesn't exist. If you rent your permission list 200 times a year, you could generate enough revenue to figure out if this is a program you'd like to install.

COMPILATION METHODS

This Home-Based business model is designed to collect names solely from sources, age 18 and over, who have given their written permission to be included on your Permission Lists. They will complete and submit their signed Consumer Data Form, including a Reverse Residual (optional) for the sole purpose of receiving offers from retailers (akin to a Buyers' Club) for goods and services but at a deeper discount than has been made to the general public in previously marketing offers. Retailers will identify those consumers on your Permission List as (Example: Kodel Group Members) creating a meeting of the minds for what it is expected and what is being offered as a result of their active participation in this particular Buyers' Club.

Brokers will at all times, maintain source documents of permission granted for each new member lending their name and consumer information.

Brokers will devise their own marketing strategies for attracting names.

Brokers are **prohibited** from engaging in random data collection practices to include, but not limited to, public records, telephone directories, internet spamming, as none of these constitute permission or provide a source document.

SEEDING

Seeding a mailing list is a common practice used to monitor unauthorized use and to protect the seller as specified in the terms of the *Use Agreement*. As a Permission List Broker, you may wish to employ this technique to track your lists.

Surely you've heard on the news at one time or another where someone's cat received a large refund check or outrageous bill. That's sort of how seeding works. You can bet that cat isn't done receiving offers!

Basically, for each list you rent you *'plant'* coded names or misleading spellings or initials but with a correct address so you can receive that mailing back. Then later, if these names reappear in subsequent mailings you can track them back to the original source—the (client) you rented your list to. Seed each list differently.

The prices of your rented lists are also based on the number of uses. If a client pays for a one-time use, and then violates the terms of your agreement by using them again, or worse yet, resells them to other companies, you have a legitimate claim—from breach of contract to intellectual property infringement. If you are so inclined, you can file for damages because they have either reused or sold your list (without your permission) to other companies who then profited.

Whatever you decide you must protect your lists & hold whoever violates the terms of your Use Agreement accountable. This is the very means in which you earn your living. They are stealing your product. So protect your lists. Protect yourself. Protect your business.

WORK PRODUCT

The broker/compiler shall maintain title and ownership to any permission lists, they produce to include mailing labels, magnetic tapes, manifests or proof list. Compiled names, addresses, buying preferences, income levels, etc., are considered proprietary *'Work Product'* and therefore the property of the compiling Broker. Brokers may transfer ownership of their permission lists to businesses who 'buy' their lists outright or as otherwise determined.

Furthermore, permission lists constitute a 'trade secret' due to their confidential nature and compilation methods. Disclosures to third parties outside the scope of the Broker must have in force a signed *'Use Agreemen'''* by the owning Broker stating the intended use and terms of sale or rental.

Unless agreed to as set forth in the 'Use Agreement' no customer or client is permitted to reproduce, copy, or otherwise duplicate a Broker's Permission List. Generally, lists are rented on a one-time usage basis but may be negotiated for multiply uses by the owning Broker.

RED HOT TIPS

SUCCESSFUL USERS OF MAILING LISTS

Appliance Retailers

Baby & Juvenile Furniture Retailers
Banks
Beauty Salons
Bicycle Dealers
Business Schools

Carpet & Rug Cleaners/Retailers
Children & Infant Wear Retailers
Churches
Colleges & Universities
Computer Retailers

Day Care Centers
Dentists
Department Stores
Dog & Cat Centers
Drug Stores

Financial Advisors/Consultants
Fingernail Salons
Florists
Food Planners
Furniture Retailers

Garden Centers
Gift Shops
Grocery Stores

Hairstyling Salons
Hardware Retailers
Health Clubs
Home Centers
Hospitals

Insurance Agents
Interior Decorators/Designers
Investment Managers

Jewelry Retailers

Lawn Care Companies

Magazine Publishers
Maternity Stores
Medical Professionals
Mortgage Lenders

Newspaper Publishers
Nursing Homes

Optometrists

Pest Control Companies
Pet Supply Retailers
Photographers
Photo Finishers
Physicians

Radio Stations
Realtors
Restaurants
Retirement Communities

Security System Dealers
Stock & Bond Brokers

Trade & Technical Schools

Veterinarians

Water Treatment Services

Attention Permission List Brokers: This ought to get you pointed in the right direction on who exactly to contact when you're ready to begin renting your exclusive Permission Lists. But in no way is this a complete list of businesses that rent mailing lists. These are only *categories*. Like, '*Restaurants.*' How many restaurants are in your community alone? We can say with confidence, you'll never run out of companies to rent your permission lists to. Bon appetite.

USE AGREEMENT
(Permission Lists)

Made this _____day of _____ 20___ between (Your Company), herein

called the 'Agency' and _____, hereinafter called the

'Customer and/or Client.'

Terms and Conditions:

1. The Agency, serving as broker & national compiler, makes available to the Client, our exclusive Permission Lists, as set forth in the terms of this agreement, as follows:

2. The Agency as an independent broker, shall maintain title to all permission lists, source documents and systems of records, mailing labels, magnetic tapes, transcripts, 3x5 sales lead cards, manifests or proof lists granted herein. The Permission List, which the Agency agrees to supply, is for the Customer's use for the expressed purpose agreed upon as stated in this agreement, and will not be sold, re-sold, rented, re-rented, shared, or used in any other way.

3. The Client agrees this particular Permission List is for **Stated Purpose**:

    _____

4.   ✓ The Customer agrees the Agency's Permission List is for:
    { } one-time use only
    { } _____uses
    { } unlimited uses (for a one-year period) – Dates: _____

5. The Agency will provide Client a Permission List in the following format:

    [ ] 3x5 Sales Lead Cards

[ ] Mailing Labels
 ( ) Pressure Sensitive (Peel & Stick)
 ( ) Cheshire (Ungummed Labels for automated machinery)
[ ] Prospect Lists (Used for Sales Planning or Telemarketing)
[ ] Diskette (3.5 or 5.5 sizes for any IBM compatible or MAC)
[ ] Magnetic Tape.
[ ]   CD Rom (IBM or MAC compatible)
[ ] Email List
[ ] Other: _____

6.   Customer agrees _not_ to replicate / duplicate Permission List or use list to supplement other mailing lists, either in whole or in part. Client acknowledges the Agency _seeds_ their lists to monitor unauthorized use.

7.   Client agrees to identify The Agency's permission list members in their mailings or offers as '**Kodel Group Members**.' [Example Only]

8.   While the Agency makes every attempt to provide _100% accurate & current_ Permission Lists as a matter of company policy, The Agency cannot be held responsible for inaccuracies or errors in information provided by consumers. The Agency cannot therefore be held liable or accountable for, and makes no guarantees or promises to subsequent response rates or deliverability of our Permission Lists.

9.   That said, **100%** of the Agency's members, on this Permission List, have given their expressed written permission & signature to be solicited by you, the Client. Moreover, members have agreed to be _more receptive_ of offers and **_99.6 %_**, have _paid_ to be added to our Permission Lists.

10.   The Agency maintains Permission List Grantors' consumer preferences, habits, hobbies, income range, renter/owner status, current mailing address, within our 'work product - trade secret' of highly confidential and privileged source documents for verification purposes on a limited, random sampling case by case bases.

11.   Suffice it to say, members have given their permission, paid an amount to the Agency to join our Permission Lists, lent their names & provided _whatever consumer information about themselves they deemed appropriate._ They do so, as a means of eliminating for you, the Client, making '_cold calls_' or '_unsolicited_' mailings saving your marketing dollars.

12. Client acknowledges the Agency provides a captive audience for them. An exclusive *'buyers club'* where members fully expect to receive their offers at _deeper_ discounts than would normally be offered to the general public in a _traditional_ direct mail advertising campaign. Client agrees to offer _____% discount to our micro-targeted Permission List membership.

13. If undeliverable mail / email exceeds 10% of a Permission List order, the Agency will refund the Client ____ cents per piece over 10%. The Agency values your business & wants to keep you as a loyal/repeat customer. Our lists will prove themselves as a valuable business tool by generating sales. Undeliverable mail pieces or email confirmation must be received by the Agency by certified, return receipt mail (or alternative agreed to method) within 90 days of our Use Agreement date. Refunds will be made within 30 days after receipt or credited to Client's subsequent list rentals as agreed.

14. Client acknowledges the Agency's lists constitute a _highly proprietary_ trade secret containing confidential information, which has been disclosed to the Client for their sole use as described herein. Client agrees not to share information or lists with third parties. (Initial: _____)

15. Client agrees to hold harmless and indemnify the Agency against any and all claims, actions, liabilities, losses, expenses, and penalties relating to any wrongful disclosure of information, intellectual property, invasion of privacy or the violation of any civil rights of any person claiming the same with respect to the Permission List used by this Customer or any breach uses attributed to this Client in contradiction to this Use Agreement.

16. Client further agrees that in the event the Client violates any of the terms and conditions set forth in this Rental Use Agreement, or violates a moral clause by engaging in unauthorized or unlawful uses of permission lists, such as, but not limited to pornography or spamming, the Client will pay the Agency, in addition to damages, all court costs and legal fees that the Agency, may incur under the terms and conditions of this agreement.

17a. Client agrees to pay ABC *either:*_____cents per name based on_ # _____ Names for <u>One Use</u> or #_____of uses. **Total order price** of $_____ is due prior to receipt of Permission Lists Names/Addresses.

OR

17b. As a *Negotiated* volume *set price* for #_____Names/Addresses for number of uses # _____ a **Total Invoice Order** of $ _____ is due prior to receipt of Permission Lists.

ATTEST:

DATE: _____   DATE: _____

_____   _____
For the Agency   For the Client

_____   _____
Print Name   Print Name

LIABILITY

Your liability as a list broker is something you need to be aware. Before you rent or sell any names, you may wish to contact the Direct Marketing Association (DMA) to obtain further information they have available.

For example, the DMA guidelines state that list professionals should ascertain the nature of a mailing list's intended use _before_ providing it. As a List Broker, you may share responsibility if your lists are used inappropriately, illegally.

The **best advice** we can give here is to be smart. Know to whom you're selling your lists to. Are the businesses reputable? Exercise good common sense. There will be plenty of demand for you lists, so make sound judgments not hasty or greedy ones. This really isn't a problem with the larger, well-known, established companies—even those smaller businesses in your local community are fine.

We **highly advise** <u>not</u> selling lists to any unknown, unverified individuals or companies from the internet. Unsolicited spamming is reaching epidemic proportions. This has become a cesspool of inappropriate business practices and outright scams and **you could become liable** for _their_ actions.

Just make sound business decisions and you'll be fine.

DISCLAIMER

This publication provides the author's sole opinions with respect to the subject matter contained herein. Neither the author nor the publisher intends to render legal, tax, accounting or other professional advice. The author and publisher make no warrants, guarantees, or promises for the presented conceptual thesis.

Should the reader become an Independent List Broker/Compiler or Associate Member, it is suggested you seek, when necessary, the services of appropriate licensed professionals with respect to licensing of a business or sole proprietorship or any other legal, accounting or tax decisions. Comply with all local, state, county and federal laws and all licensing requirements for the community in which you live or conduct business.

Consideration should also be given to laws and regulations, which are administered by other federal agencies, such as the Federal Trade Commission, as well as other relevant laws or regulations in various states and local jurisdictions.

The publisher and author disclaims any personal liability, loss or risk incurred as a consequence of the use or implementation, either directly or indirectly, of any advice, information, or methods presented herein. Sadly, in our litigious society, the aforementioned disclaimer is necessary as neither the publisher nor author have direct supervisory control over the actions of independent brokers or associate members or how this information is implemented, applied or otherwise disseminated.

Each Broker/Compiler & Associate Member agrees to take full and complete responsibility for _their_ own actions, code of conduct, moral and ethical measures and principles, holding the publisher and author harmless for any claims, including liability, property damage, personal injury, loss or risk incurred as a consequence of the use, implementation or application of this material whether directly or indirectly, of any advice, direction, guidance, information or methods presented in this _Home-Based Business Model for Success_.

This agreement shall be deemed to have beeen entered into and shall be governed by and interpreted in accordance with the laws of the State of Oregon applicable to agreements executed and fully carried out within Oregon. Any action, proceedings or litigation concerning this material, may only be brought in Josephine County, Oregon. You agree that the courts of Josephine County, Oregon shall have exclusive jurisdiction over you. You agree that any disputes or controversies arising under or relating to this agreement or any of its terms, or any effort by any party to enforce, interpret, construe, rescind, terminate or annul this agreement, or any provision thereof, and any and all disputes or controversies arising under or relating to implementing this business model, shall be resolved by binding arbitration.

LIFE RULES

(Character Still Matters)

Hope is NOT a Strategy

Think Beyond the Act
(Actions May Have Dire Consequences)

Be Prepared

Be Prompt

Be Patient

Engage

Show Respect

Be Honest

Be Responsible

Be Considerate

Be Dependable

Dream

Believe

Act

MORAL CLAUSE

Brokers will _not_ provide (rent/share/sell/give/transfer or make available) their permission lists arbitrarily or capriciously to any individual, agency, telemarketer or company, including over the internet to anyone which is considered questionable, of poor reputation, character or means. Brokers must protect individuals' information on their lists from receiving unsavory unsolicited offers. Brokers are expressly prohibited from providing their lists to companies, entities or individuals wherein a _reasonable person_ (under the law) may deem such action offensive, objectionable or otherwise in poor taste. As an example, but not limited to, your permission lists _will not_ be provided to pornographers.

BUSINESS LICENSE

As a general rule, cities and counties may not require a business license for this particular home-based business, though they may require a Home Occupations Permit. You'll have to check with your local business-licensing department for specifics. Costs vary.

CONDITIONS OF PERMIT

In granting permits, cities are mostly concerned with the noise, traffic, visual or odor impact a business generates. They are interested whether or not you have signs, weekly deliveries or clients. Inventory concerns are not a problem for your list business. Cities are primarily interested in seeing that the residential character is being maintained. Your brokerage business is done in the privacy of your own home via the telephone, internet, email or mail. Once you begin renting your lists, you may have to file an assumed business name with your city/state.

ASSUMED BUSINESS NAME

File an assumed business name with your Secretary of State, Corporation Division, Business Registry Department. Costs vary.

CRITICALLY IMPORTANT

If you choose to list your social security number on your state assumed business name registration form, *it will become part of the public record available to any party upon request!* The form may ask for your social security number, but only as an *option*. Let common sense prevail here!

BUSINESS TYPE

You will have to decide what is best for your business—sole proprietorship, Limited Liability Company (LLC), incorporation, partnership, etc.

S.I.C.

Standard Industrial Classifications (S.I.C.) Code. When applying for an assumed business name, DBA (doing business as) you will have to include an S.I.C. Select one that most closely identifies your business. Advertising: 7310; Management Consulting 7392, Mailing 7330, Computer & Data Processing Services 7370, etc.

STATUS QUO
WHAT YOU SHOULD KNOW ABOUT MAILING LISTS
BEFORE YOU MAIL

This brief overview of the _traditional mailing list environment_ & types of lists used in direct marketing is necessary for your perusal but can serve only as an introduction. Once you read this, you'll understand why we decided to build a better mousetrap. We have a lot more fun!

The four primary types of mailing lists are <u>Resident</u>, <u>Compiled Consumer</u>, <u>Compiled Business</u> & <u>Specialty Response</u>. Each list is unique, both in terms of advantages & limitations.

RESIDENT
A Resident mailing list is the most effective way to reach every household in any geographic area as it does not include an individual's name at each address but most mailers use a special salutation: '_To Our Friends At_' or '_To Our Neighbors At_.'

The term 'Resident' derived from the nature of this mailing list provides neighborhood-by-neighborhood selectivity. It is divided into the individual routes that each postal carrier delivers every day. Resident mailing lists provide household penetration for the complete advertising coverage (newspaper advertising provides only 50% to 60% penetration). Resident lists also qualify for the lowest possible postal rate, an important consideration for every mailing.

Resident lists can be targeted at housing types (homes, apartments & in some areas, mobile homes). '<u>Feathering</u>' & '<u>nth</u>' selection techniques (mailing to every other household or predetermined sequence of households) further enhances selectivity & flexibility.)

Of particular importance is the fact that Resident lists are 100% deliverable as addresses validated by the U.S. Postal Service—and are not dependent upon the name of an individual living at an address...or...Current Resident.

With the available statistics, Resident mailing lists can be generated with complete demographic selectivity by a complete list of variables.

<u>Typical of the selections available are</u>:

> Average household income
> Percent income from investments
> Percent professional, technical, managerial
> Dominant ethnic group code
> Percent households with children
> Percent motor vehicle ownership
> Average Car Value
> Single family homes or Multi-family dwelling units

Special Spending Index Groups (SIG) also rate consumers spending habits of residents in each Carrier Route. For instance, routes with above average spending for food away from home (fast food) or sundry items can be selected. Spending Index Groups (all still quite general in nature) are available for:

1) Groceries; drug & sundry items
2) Food away from home - restaurants
3) Discount; furniture; hardware stores
4) Financial; Electronics; Major appliances
5) Catalog showrooms; Jewelry
6) Tires, batteries & accessories
7) Entertainment

Direct Marketing members of the National Association of Advertising Distributors (NAAD) can make available to its customers statistical and selectivity data on resident lists comprising more than 85 million households throughout the nation.

COMPILED CONSUMER

These lists are compiled from sources including telephone directories, automobile registration files, driver's license files, product warranty cards, & other proprietary sources. The lists are *as accurate as their sources*. This means the ultimate deliverability of the mail can vary depending upon time of last updating, geographic area & selectivity. The ability to target a mailing is greatly enhanced by the use of a Compiled Consumer list. Variables such as age, income, length of residence, gender, type of dwelling unit and other selections are household specific. Other selections include marital status, number of children under 18 in household, and even the make and model of an automobile owned.

Income selectors are available in basic groupings:

Under $15,000 a year	$15,000+	$25,000+
$35,000+	$50,000+	$75,000+

It is important to note that income assignments for each household are based on a complex computer-based formula model and in no way implies a totally accurate statement of family income. Generally, the income estimates are considered conservative and are best used only as a relative guide to income groupings. The combinations of selections are many, widely varied and are selected to best match the target audience for product or service. A list might be selected from middle-aged adults with an estimated income of $35,000+ who have children. Another common selection might be males with an estimated income of $50,000+ who own luxury automobiles.

COMPILED BUSINESS

All business lists us Standard Industrial Classifications (SIC) codes to segment businesses into groupings by their business activity. The mailing list industry uses these individual groups so mailings can be targeted to specific types of businesses.

Business lists are compiled from telephone and industrial directories and other private and governmental sources. The firms are assigned to one (or more) SIC codes based on their primary or secondary business or businesses.

The first two digits of an SIC code defines the 10 major business groups:

01-09	Agriculture, Forestry and Fishing
10-14	Mining
15-17	Contract Construction
20-39	Manufacturing
40-49	Transportation, Communication & Utilities
50-51	Wholesale Trade
52-60	Retail Trade
61-67	Finance, Insurance & Real Estate
70-89	Services—Business and Professional
90-95	Government Offices

Third and fourth digits segment the groups more finely:

SIC 5000	segments to wholesalers
SIC 506	denotes electrical
SIC 507	identifies plumbing
SIC 5063	specifies electrical equipment
SIC 5064	specifies TV and radio

...and so on, through...

SIC 5094   Jewelry, gems and watches wholesalers

Through the use of an eight-digit system, a Business list can be highly selectable and refined. Titles usually are used to get mail to the appropriate prospect contact within the company. Typical titles would be president, general manager, office manager, vice president marketing, or any other functional title in the company. You can further refine your Business list audience by choosing the size of business, by number of employees or sales volume.

SPECIALTY RESPONSE

These lists include the broad grouping of <u>subscription</u> & <u>circulation</u> lists for magazines, owners of specific types of products, individuals who have responded to previous direct mail or space advertising solicitations, members of clubs, groups or organizations, and any other special compilations that are commercially available. **Permission Lists will likely fall under this category!**

BUSINESS OWNERS

Developing & maintaining your own customer/prospect mailing list provides a valuable sales tool. Your mailing list can be a direct, personal sales link that can lessen dependence on other advertising media & with new data processing technology, hygiene services such as ZIP-code correction, merge/purge, deduping & genderization can be applied to PC-based mailing lists.

NATIONAL CHANGE OF ADDRESS

With the 1986 introduction of the USPS *National Change of Address File (NCOA)*, all Compiled Consumer and Compiled Business lists can be updated more frequently. The computer updating provides new addresses for both individuals and companies who have entered *change-of-address* orders with the post office.

QUESTIONS & ANSWERS

Q. How rich are companies getting selling my name?
Answer: A True Success Story. American Business Information Corporation, a national mailing list complier, was started fifty years ago with just $100. Recent sales surpassed $190 million, with over 1.6 million customers! (He was one of our better students!) We're kidding. Your results will vary.

Q. How long does it take to order a mailing list?
Answer: Resident lists are produced in about four business days. Consumer & Business lists are ordered from compilers & generally take 10 days.

Q. Do I 'buy' mailing lists?
Answer: No, you only buy the medium on which the mailing list is delivered: labels, a manuscript printout, magnetic tape, CDs or 3x5 cards. All mailing lists represent proprietary information, which the owner rents to you for one-time use, unless otherwise agreed upon. Many lists can be rented for multiple uses, at a lower per use cost.

Q. Do you guarantee mailing lists?
Answer: No. Mailing list companies cannot make '**response rate**' guarantees but do strive to achieve a very high rate of deliverability.

Q. How accurate are mailing lists?
Answer: The accuracy of all mailing lists varies. Lists that are updated from the telephone directory can only be as accurate as the directory itself. Telephone directories go out-of-date at the rate of 2% to 3% or more a month depending upon the geographic area. While updates are available from other sources, lists do become outdated. A mailing list, which is 85% to 95% deliverable, is considered a 'clean' mailing list.

Q. Can I order a mailing list on my own?
Answer: Yes, although you may find that many list compilers will release their lists only to a recognized mail marketing company.

Q. May I copy the labels to use again?
Answer: No, labels are for one-time use only and are seeded with coded names to protect against unauthorized multiple uses.

Q. How much to mailing lists cost?
Answer: Prices may vary greatly depending upon types of lists, quantity of names ordered, selectivity specified and minimum order required.

A telemarketing list for example, may cost $10,000. American Home & Remodeling or Milgard manufacturing, both window and siding companies, have established call centers and use telemarketing lists. It may take 300 to 400 calls to set *'one'* appointment. One reason for this unsolicited low response is because these are 'cold' calls. The expenses are great. Telemarketers can earn $15+hr.

Q. What is the 'error factor' on mailing lists?
Answer: Major list compilers strive for complete accuracy, but again, accuracy depends on the type of list, source data, last updating & geographic area. *Resident lists are the most deliverable*. Consumer & Business lists can have error factors as high as 10% to 15% or even higher depending upon when the list was last updated. Specialty lists can range from very accurate magazine subscription lists to out-of-date lists. Strive to keep your Permission Lists highly accurate/updated.

Q. Is there any type of contract when renting a list?
Answer: Yes. A list Rental Use Agreement with details, terms and conditions of your list rented is entered into and signed before a list is ordered.

NOTE:
A *sample* 'Use Agreement' is provided at page 83.

ACKNOWLEDGMENTS

The Author would like to thank the following people or organizations for their contributing efforts:

Lynn Kraudelt, Personnel Administrator, The United States Olympic Training Center, Colorado Springs, CO for mailing list information with respect to their fund raising efforts.

John J. Gawrysiak, M.B.A., Lt. Colonel, USAF (Ret), Tampa, FL for layout design, logo, format & software support.

Mitchell Guy Shepard, Grants Pass, OR for 'The Mitchell Factor' perspective.

Harvard Business School for the paper on 'Network' Marketing.

The United States Postal Service for their Small Business Assistance & Direct Mail Delivers manuals with Case Studies & the United States Postal Inspection Service for your letters, guidance & information.

CBS Television Network for transcripts on CBS This Morning, with Harry Smith and Paula Zahn regarding guest, Ram Avrahami on the topic of his mailing list lawsuit against, U.S. News & World Report.

Dan Armstrong, Brookings, OR owner of Bug-E-Boyz Pest Control & telemarketing client of CenturyLink marketing lists.

CASE STUDIES

BLOOMINGDALE'S

CUSTOMER LOYALTY

At Bloomingdale's _targeted mailings_ are a way of life!

Each year, the $1.6 _billion_ dollar upscale retailer deploys **over 55 million** personalized pieces in _550 distinct Direct Mail promotions_ for their 21 stores.

Sending multiple mailings affords Bloomingdale's the luxury of 'talking' to different segments of shoppers. _They can identify, customize & deliver highly relevant messages_. As a result, response rates to their best customer segments have risen to 25-30%. Targeted mailings also enable Bloomingdale's to successfully reach marginal audiences like lapsed customers. By treating them special & sending them unique offers, they can reactivate customers at a profitable response rate.

Survey results <u>confirm</u> **Bloomingdale's customers prefer mailings** to other advertising. Nine out of ten say they would rather read something mailed directly to them. Why? Survey says: because they feel they might miss an important sales message otherwise.

What underpins this success is the company's <u>cutting edge database</u> marketing efforts—& expert use of _prized customer information_. Skillfully employing modeling, segmentation & demographic analysis to define their audiences, Bloomingdale's tailors precise mailings that promote long-range retention & advance customers up the loyalty ladder.

While other retailers face shrinking margins, Bloomingdale's phenomenal growth is in full bloom. Its profitable customer database has expanded to twice the size it was just four years prior. It is a model for the industry. <u>As a result of more precisely targeted mailings</u>, Bloomingdale's Return on Investment (ROI) has improved by as much as 30%.

<u>Bottom line</u>: **Mailing lists generate sales! Permission Lists will eclipse them!**

GENERAL MOTORS

GENIUS BUSINESS MODEL

General Motors (GM) executives were seeking ways to increase sales of cars & trucks, and increase customer loyalty. The result is arguably one of the most intriguing & instructive marketing tales of all time.

To create loyalty & the sales they were after, GM decided on a novel approach: *they would offer a GM MasterCard to consumers.* Consumers would *accumulate credits* enabling them to enjoy discounts on new GM vehicles. In addition to any sales prompted by the discounts, GM would, as a bonus, enjoy additional profits, as a MasterCard partner. How did GM pinpoint prospects for such an 'offer'? Would you believe **Mailing Lists?**

GM *carefully* selected 30 million households for their mailing launch. While the 30-million number may suggest a 'mass mailing' in fact, this was a carefully targeted mailing going *only to addresses scrupulously selected as suitable prospects.*

GM's first mailing dropped in September 1992 & *marketing history was made*! Some three million new GM MasterCard accounts were booked in the first three months—a Response Rate of 10%. Nine months later, by the middle of 1993, some six million GM cardholders had charged more than $7 billion dollars! (Still don't think the mailing list industry is BIG BUSINESS?) Industry analysts consider it the most successful credit card launch ever executed. More importantly, the effort worked precisely as it had been intended. More than 25,000 cardholders redeemed their GM card earnings toward the purchase of a new GM car or truck. As these vehicles aged over the next seven years, consumers would presumably continue to use their GM MasterCards & accumulate more points, which is a strong incentive to replace their present cars & trucks with GM products.

There are a multitude of lessons to be learned here. One, the power of mail to targeted consumers & deliver of a powerful, detailed sales pitch. Another was the *imaginative* way in which **mailing lists** were used. It took true nonlinear thinking, as well as daring innovation to achieve these truly outstanding results. Once you're established as a Permission List Broker, even the corporate giants will come looking for your Permission Lists because businesses are always hungry.

HALLMARK

CARDS & MORE

How important is a *long-term relationship* in business? To Hallmark Cards, a company with a 100+ year history of helping people build & maintain strong personal relationships, it's synonymous with success.

Hallmark's millions of **Gold Crown Card members** spend on average 70% *more per store visit than* nonmembers. The frequent shopper rewards program is comprised of personalized newsletters & solo *mailings*, with retail traffic incentives & point award statements based on store purchasing behavior. *The program has exceeded every benchmark* set for it in terms of its sign-up rate; **double-digit response rates** to retail incentives & the amount of money customers spend as members.

The development of the *Gold Crown database* provided the perfect venue to further meet the needs of customers & drive additional store traffic. The *greeting card leader* took its success in relationship marketing one step further—to business clients. Creating a unit called *Business Expressions*, Hallmark now produces customized cards for businesses to use for *acquiring & retaining customers* & employees. Again, Direct Mail was an integral part of the marketing plan.

Today, Hallmark's clients span multiple industries. Whether it's a car dealership sending a 'birthday' greeting for a customer's car on the anniversary of purchase, or an insurance company recognizing a customer who's entering a new life stage, Business Expressions cards send the same, consistent message of goodwill & personal warmth.

What does all this prove? A little **innovative** *relationship marketing* can go a long way & have a high-impact. Well-timed Direct Mail program can deliver lasting value.

Note
We are striving to achieve an innovative marketing relationship turning the the traditional mailing list industry on its ear…with our Permission Lists.

HARRY & DAVID

BEAR CREEK CORPORATION

It was the Depression that made Harry & David turn to direct mail in the first place. Their father had built a booming business selling rare Royal Riviera pears from his orchard in Medford, Oregon. But when the Depression came along, it ruined the European luxury pear market. Harry & David realized they had to find new markets for their fruit, fast!

In 1935, Harry traveled east to New York while David went south to San Francisco, each taking several crates of pears. They called on every VIP they could think of, to get them to sample the pears. When they cam back to Oregon, they had stacks of orders for their fruit, which they mailed out in time for Christmas.

Despite their initial success, Harry & David realized that calling on people personally was an uneconomical way to sell fruit. They had to find something more efficient. The following year, they fortuitously decided to <u>sell through the mail</u>, creating a small catalog of their pears. It was mailed to all the people they'd called on the year before, and many others as well. Soon, the orders they had been hoping for came pouring in.

Impressed by the mail's ability to generate Christmas orders, Harry & David started looking for a way to expand their business, making it less seasonal. Two years later, in 1938, they launched a <u>revolutionary concept</u>, the Fruit-of-the-Month Club. It was the first of its kind and the inspiration for all sorts of other continuity clubs.

In 1964, they again expanded their year-round business when they bought Jackson & Perkins, a rose-and-horticulture mail-order company.

It is the predictability of mail that grew their business. It is this use of <u>mailing lists</u> that allowed them to expand their mail-order business profitably. Catalog mailings are not affected by external conditions, like a blizzard, which can keep people home and stores closed. By studying and analyzing their mail-order sales, Harry & David have been able to expand in a logical, consistent manner.

Direct mail has helped Harry & David grow from a single orchard into <u>the country's largest</u> fresh fruit and gourmet foods mail-order business.

Today, they sell cakes and cookies from their own bakery, candy from their kitchens, as well as peaches and pears from their many orchards. Recently, they've even expanded into a lifestyle catalog, which carries various items from the Pacific Northwest, such as clothing and accessories.

<u>Note</u>
The Author spent four months working in Customer Service learning what he could. His research revealed a truly quality company who made $600,000,000 in sales during one holiday season alone. Six hundred million! Now that's a lot of loyal customers calling in their holiday orders. You might be one of them.

Interesting though, how a small, local company grew so large and became so successful that Tokyo-based Yamanouchi Pharmaceutical Company owned it until April 2004. Wasserstein & Co., LP, a privately held investment firm with offices in New York, Los Angeles and Palo Alto next acquired The Bear Creek Corporation.

<u>**You gotta love those Mailing Lists.**</u>

Now, if you had to venture an educated guess: How valuable do you think their mailing list is to others hoping to attract customers willing to buy products online? Do you think they sell (rent) their lists?

If you recall earlier in the material, this is called a by-product of their main business.

You have to believe tens, nay, hundreds of thousands of businesses, if not millions nationwide, also believe in mailing lists. Once you begin offering them your Buyers' Club Permission Lists, you too can rise in this industry.

LEVI STRAUSS

SUGAR & SPICE & EVERYTHING NICE

To increase interest in the Fall *back-to-school line* of Levi's Jeans for Girls, a direct mail campaign was <u>targeted</u> at girls in the 7 to 11-year old group.

Levi Strauss & Co., *with the help of a direct response agency*, decided upon a retail **co-op strategy**. A customized mailing was developed & sent to *girls in the target age range* within a 7.5-mile radius of the retailer's stores.

To bring customers into the stores, an ***involvement device*** was chosen. In this case, it was there intriguing puzzles that featured photos of the Levi's Jeans for Girls line. Girls could complete the puzzles, and then bring them into the store to qualify to win a free trip to Walt Disney World.

In addition to generating a high level of interest, the mailing program generated more than 7% response & doubled brand awareness within the target group.

Notes

Involvement devices actively engage the consumer and can be as simple as a scratch off lottery ticket or as involving as answering <u>survey questions</u>.

Our *Consumer Form* example is also considered an 'involvement device.' Buyers' Club Members: Complete them with care, so our Brokers can expand their client base with enough accurate information to bring you great offers and most importantly for Brokers, a premium price for their Permission Lists.

OMAHA STEAKS

BRANDED

Omaha Steaks branded themselves through direct mail.

In 1917, nobody had a clue about mail-order meat, not even the Simon family. When J.J. & his son, B.A. Simon opened the _Table Supply Meat Company_, their goal was clear: to supply the best Midwestern USDA corn-fed beef to grocery stores & restaurants.

However, by 1952, that began to change. By then, the Simons were receiving calls from friends elsewhere saying, "Yes, the weather's fine, but we miss the midwestern beef...so could you please send some?" After enough of these calls, they decided to mail a small brochure to local residents offering beef shipping and in 1966, under the name **Omaha Steaks International**, they mailed their first national catalog.

But creating awareness takes more than a nice catalog & great steak. _You need to find customers_. So Omaha Steaks prospected a little. They researched exactly who their best consumers were. This allowed them to _develop accurate consumer models_ & **purchase _mailing lists_**.

Omaha Steaks now acquires 90% of their new customers through direct mail and of course, the internet. They keep customers by continually mailing or emailing new offers. Today, Omaha Steaks serves over 1.2 million customers through the mail & at their 33 outlet stores. This makes them the largest direct response marketer of steaks & other frozen gourmet foods in the country. **Before they started using direct mail, they were a family with a dream. And some steaks to sell.**

Note

Are you hungry for your piece of pie now? Hey Brokers, think Omaha Steaks might be interested in your Buyers' Club Permission Lists? Don't wait for the cows to come home...find out!

TRAVELERS

GOING MY WAY

Travelers Property Casualty recognized a need to increase customer loyalty and decrease attrition rates among its auto and homeowner policyholders. They recognized policyholders are more likely to defect during the first three years as a customer.

Attrition rates were up to 17.5%. So a program was developed to be time-targeted, individualized, and able to produce real, bottom-line results. _Mail was the only medium that fit all criteria needed to make the program successful_. Approximately 20 different mail pieces were created for their One to One program, which included a mixture of newsletters, seasonal mailers, renewal reminders & thank-you notes.

Each piece focuses on a specific customer need and can be customized with the agent's name, address and logo. Agents are able to make appropriate direct mail selections for each of their customers. Agents can tailor mailings to the individual and time them according to a customer's policy renewal date.

Agents have seen an increase in policyholder retention and experienced an average **389% return on investment** (ROI).

Note

What you're seeing here is how direct mail impacts a company's bottom-line. As Buyers' Club Permission List members, by giving your permission and inviting companies to solicit you personally, with deep discounts, well, that's a win-win, good for businesses & you! It's also good for Brokers wanting to create and run their own Home-Based Broker Business!

USAA

BANK WITHOUT COOKIES

The USAA Federal Savings Bank (FSB) has no lobby, no teller windows, and no branches. On the plus side, count $6+ billion in assets and more than 2 million satisfied customers worldwide.

USAA FSB is descended from the United Services Automobile Association, formed in the 1920s to provide affordable insurance to military officers, a highly mobile group, but always reachable by mail.

Over the years, USAA included civilians in their customer base and added new mail order financial services. From the beginning, the bank has relied on mail to conduct business & Direct Mail to consistently generate revenue. One example, in 1996, a direct mail campaign was needed to stimulate inactive credit card holders during the holiday season.

The 'offer' was to get members to use their USAA credit cards just three times between Thanksgiving and year's end and receive a free 30-minute prepaid phone card. The projected break-even point was a three-time credit card usage for each member with purchases of $70. **The mailing generated an outstanding return.** Customers used their cards an average of 11 times & bought $900 worth of goods. NONE OF THIS is possible with outdated mailing addresses.

Even in this day & age of the internet, Direct Mail is still a great marketing tool because it not only lets companies measure return on their investment (ROI) it helps to improve upon it. While you might feel somewhat manipulated by these tactics, it's how businesses stimulate consumers into making purchases. It's the Name of the Game... Besides, you know algorithms are doing the same thing tracking your every click. We have tried to devise a way for you to profit too.

Note: We hope these Case Studies are enlightening & interesting for you. We also hope by now, you can see just how important mailing lists are to businesses. We trust you can see the potential in Permission Lists!

WINDSOR VINEYARDS

MORE WINE MY DEAR

Windsor Vineyards, located in Sonoma County, California, is the nation's leading direct marketer of wine. Not only do they grow their own grapes and produce their wine, they also provide personalized wine labels for their customers.

In 1959, they launched a comprehensive marketing program that continues today. They attribute their success to the use of integrated direct communications, which includes direct mail & telemarketing programs.

Windsor uses direct mail to conduct surveys. As they learnt more about their customers, they were able to send out relevant & timely offers. As a result, they've increased loyalty & lifted response rates as high as 14%.

Windsor has seen aggressive growth over the years, which confirms their belief in the power of direct marketing. They intend to continue this comprehensive approach of keeping their current customers and growing their customer base.

Note

As a Permission List Broker, trust your instincts when we say, this company & many others will be very interested in your permission lists & pay handsomely for them. Cheers!

Clink

'To Your Success as a Permission List Broker!'